CHIP CARVING

**Expert Techniques and
50 All-Time Favorite Projects
The Best of *Woodcarving Illustrated Magazine***

The Best of **SCROLLSAW**
Woodworking & Crafts Magazine

CHIP CARVING

**Expert Techniques and
50 All-Time Favorite Projects
The Best of *Woodcarving Illustrated Magazine***

**From the editors of
*Scroll Saw Woodworking & Crafts***

Quilt Pattern Coasters,
by Barry McKenzie, page 66

FOX CHAPEL
PUBLISHING

© 2009 by Fox Chapel Publishing Company, Inc.

Chip Carving: Expert Techniques and 50 All-Time Favorite Projects is an original work, first published in 2009 by Fox Chapel Publishing Company, Inc. The patterns contained herein are copyrighted by the authors. Readers may make copies of these patterns for personal use. The patterns themselves, however, are not to be duplicated for resale or distribution under any circumstances. Any such copying is a violation of copyright law.

ISBN 978-1-56523-449-9

Library of Congress Cataloging-in-Publication Data

   Chip carving : expert techniques and 50 all-time favorite projects /
   by the editors of Woodcarving Illustrated

       p. cm. -- (The best of woodcarving illustrated)

       Includes index

       ISBN: 978-1-56523-449-9

       1. Wood-carving. I. Wood carving illustrated.
TT199.7.C45 2009
736'.4--dc22

                 2009020991

To learn more about the other great books from Fox Chapel Publishing, or to find a retailer near you, call toll-free 800-457-9112 or visit us at *www.FoxChapelPublishing.com*.

Note to Authors: We are always looking for talented authors to write new books in our area of woodworking, design, and related crafts. Please send a brief letter describing your idea to Acquisition Editor, 1970 Broad Street, East Petersburg, PA 17520.

Printed in China
First printing: September 2009

Table of Contents

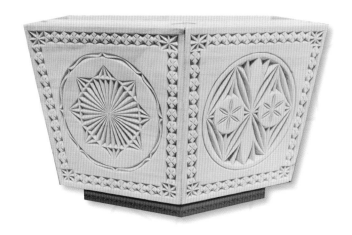

What You Can Learn

Standard chip carving, page 12

Shallow chip-carving, page 17

Old-world-style chip-carving, page 20

Free-form chip carving, page 23

Individual styles, page 26

About decorations, christmas ornament & more, page 28

What You Can Make

Snowflake ornament, page 32

Tree ornaments, page 38

Leaf ornaments, page 40

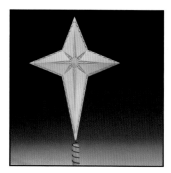

Star tree topper, page 43

Delicate icicle ornaments, page 48

Honeycomb ornaments, page 50

Delicate pierced ornaments, page 52

Angel ornaments, page 55

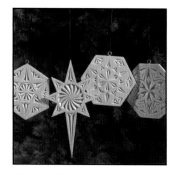

Geometric ornaments, page 57

Holiday patterns, page 59

Quilt pattern coasters, page 66

Chip carving on eggs, page 72

Landscape,
page 76

Floral chip carvings,
page 78

Chess set,
page 81

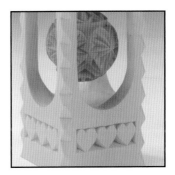

Chip carved golf balls,
page 86

Wedding plate, page 90

Chip carved letters, page 94

Colorful plaque, page 96

Classic spoon rack, page 100

Crosses, page 104

Serving tray, page 107

Mangle board, page 110

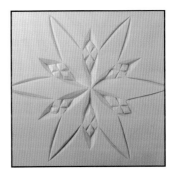

Rosette, page 114

Dove peace cross, page 115

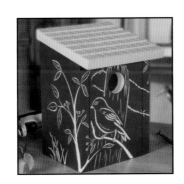

Stylish birdhouse, page 116

Teapot clock, page 122

Introduction

When asked the question, "What is chip carving, anyhow?" the standard response is: "A series of incise cuts into the wood surface that leave a design behind." But chip carving is so much more than that. Chip carving satisfies the primitive need to create something beautiful from wood. Chip carving preserves generations of tradition from master craftsmen. Chip carving expresses the unique style of each individual carver, and inspires enjoyment, whether from the carving process or admiration and use of the completed project.

Whether the wood is chip carved with the traditional geometric style, Scandinavian shallow chip, Old-World-style chip from the Netherlands, or more stylized free-form cuts, each project in this book has had a part in bringing chip carvers from the community together to share design ideas, techniques, and knowledge. Chip carvers may be few in numbers and far apart, but their passion for chip carving today will help preserve this art form for future generations to enjoy and appreciate. As you create the inspiring projects found in these pages, it is my hope that your abilities will expand—and that you will realize the many possibilities for your chip carving to reflect your own personality.

Always in the chips,
Barry McKenzie
www.chipcarvingschool.com

Wedding Plate,
by Barry McKenzie, page 90.

Chip Carving Techniques

Chip carving is a relatively safe procedure, but be sure to take any necessary precautions because you are working with very sharp knives. If you need to hold the carving in your hand with an appropriate material, or on your lap, for example, be sure to protect your hand or lap with appropriate materials, such as a carving glove or a carving apron. It's a good idea to read through the project instructions before you begin to make sure you understand everything involved. Your chip carving toolbox should generally include a chip carving knife, sandpaper, a pencil, safety tools, measuring tools of your choice, and an eraser. Unless otherwise noted, all content in this chapter was authored by Barry McKenzie.

Chip carving on eggs, page 72.

Standard Chip Carving

The standard, geometric deep chip is probably the most universally and widely used of the three styles. It is made with three equally angular and deep cuts using a chip carving knife. **Illustration 1** shows two different knife positions. Dimension A represents both the depth and the width of the chip. Angle B equals the angle of the blade entry for all three cuts. The angle usually varies between 45° and 55°.

The sequence of cuts and the position of the knife

It is not physically economical if you turn your work every time you make a stab cut. Think how time consuming it is, not to mention labor intensive, to turn the wood three times or more for every three-cornered chip. Multiply that by possibly hundreds of chips and a lot of energy is expended. Using the traditional method for making geometric chips, you only have to turn the board once.

The pearwood box with lid is the work of Lenny Benemerito, Genoa, Italy.

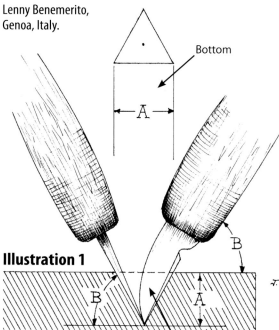

Illustration 1

A equals the depth and width of the chip. B equals the angle of entry for the knife. The first cut acts as a stop cut that determines the depth of the common bottom. Note that this three-cornered chip requires just three stab cuts. If slivers of wood are left at the bottom of the chip, it is because the cuts did not converge precisely.

The best way to create the geometric chip is to make a single change in how you hold the knife while turning the project only once.

To cut side 1: Pull the knife toward your body. The knife is gripped so that the thumb is beside the blade while resting or anchored on the wood. This has you cutting diagonally across the grain.

For side 2: Turn the board around 180° just this one time. Hold the knife with the thumb on the back of the knife in the back-cut position and cut away from your body. The cut is also made diagonally across the grain.

For side 3: Go back to the grip you used for side 1 and cut across the grain. Turning the project is not necessary.

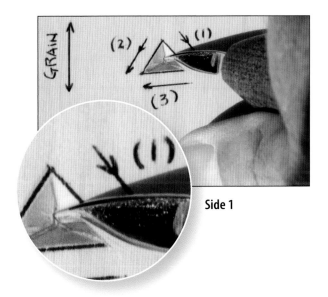

Side 1

Side 2

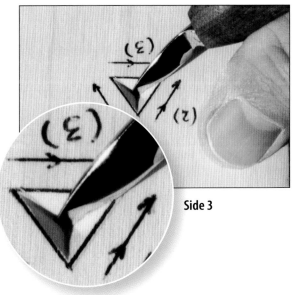

Side 3

The basswood clock was carved by Gil Steele of Knox, Pennsylvania.

The basswood plate is by Buddy Jent of Bowling Green, Kentucky.

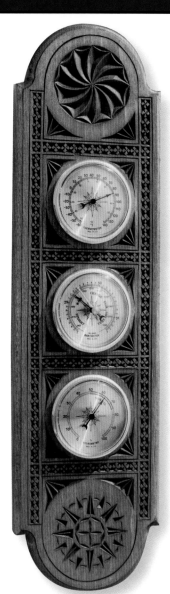

Don Deitz of Belleville, Illinois, carved the stained basswood weather station.

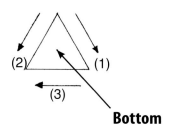

Bottom

For right-handed chip carvers

Grain

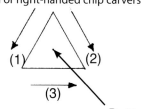

Bottom

For left-handed chip carvers

Illustration 2 shows there is a difference between how a right- and left-handed chip carver make the cuts. A right-hander makes the first cut on the right side of the triangle (with one apex pointing away from the body), the second cut on the left, and the third cut from right to left. The left-hander cuts the left side of the triangle first, then the right side, and the third cut from left to right.

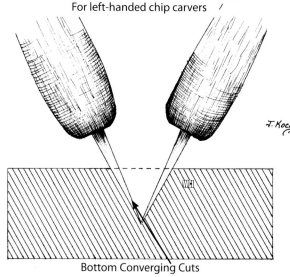

Bottom Converging Cuts

CHIP CARVING WISDOM

I have heard it said that chip carving is very easy to learn, but difficult to master. Since there are a variety of methods and styles to learn, master one technique at a time.

When I'm asked to give a simple definition of chip carving, I think of one word: converge.

The basic, geometric deep chip can be applied to a variety of shapes and sizes. All of the projects shown were winners at the 1998 Second Annual All Chip Carvers Show held in Lebanon, Missouri.

Darwin Krueger of Grinnell, Iowa, made the six-sided open box. Constructed from basswood, it sits on a short pedestal, also chip-carved.

Simple Face

by Jim Calder

Practice making standard chips with this simple project.

Roughing out the face

1 **Cut the first triangle.** Draw a line on the corner of the blank for the brow line. Cut straight in at that line with a knife to make a stop cut. Move down a bit and carve up to the line, removing a triangular chip to create the eye and cheek area.

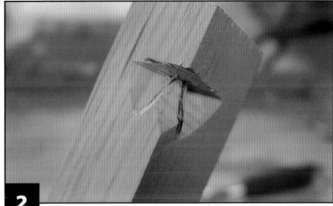

2 **Carve the cheeks.** Draw two sides of a triangle with the point of the triangle centered on the brow line. Stop-cut along the lines and carve up to the stop cuts from the sides to separate the nose from the cheeks.

3 **Outline the base of the nose.** Draw a line at the bottom of the nose; then extend the sides of the nose triangle for the top of the mustache. Stop cut along the bottom of the nose and carve up to the stop cut with the carving knife.

4 **Outline the top of the mustache.** Stop cut along the extended lines. Cut up to the stop cuts from the outside to define the mustache and separate it from the cheeks. Taper the tip of the nose from the center out toward each cheek.

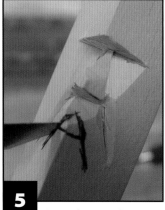

5 **Carve the mouth.** Draw another triangle as shown in the photo. Extend the side lines beyond the base. Stop cut along the sides of the triangle. Angle the knife up toward the bottom of the mustache as you cut along the base of the triangle. This will remove a chip, opening the mouth.

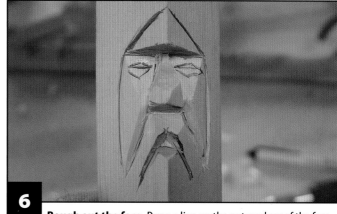

6 **Rough out the face.** Draw a line on the outer edges of the face, stop cut along the line, and make a shallow cut up to the stop cuts. Draw the forehead triangle and the eyes. The eyes are two triangles put base to base, with the bottom triangle being twice as tall as the top triangle.

Carving the details

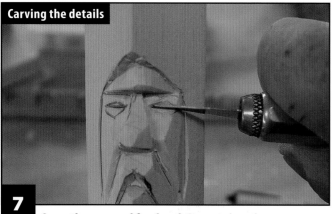

7 **Carve the eyes and forehead.** Stop cut along the common base line between the two triangles. Angle your knife and carve out the upper and lower triangles down to the stop cut. Stop cut along the top of the forehead and carve from the brow line up to the forehead using a carving knife.

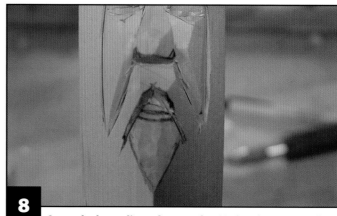

8 **Carve the lower lip and mustache.** Mark and remove small triangles on the sides of the nose to round the ball of the nose. Draw a triangle under the mouth, leaving a thin area for the lip. Stop cut along the lip and remove the triangle by cutting up to the lip using a carving knife.

9 **Add the hair and beard.** Sketch the beard and hair using the photo as a guide. Stop cut along the lines and carve up to the stop cuts from the inside. Round off the corner and add texture to the hair and beard with a V-tool. Sand and finish as desired; I suggest stain or polyurethane.

Materials & Tools

Materials:
- 2" x 2" x 5" basswood
- Stain or polyurethane (optional)
- Fine-grit sandpaper (optional)

Tools:
- Carving knife of choice
- V-tool of choice (I use a palm-style Flexcut)
- Pencil
- Paintbrush (optional)

Shallow Chip Carving

Barry McKenzie's wife Barb taught him how to play chess using his own chip carved chess set and board. Barry says he has yet to win a game.

Shallow chip carving was developed when carvers used very dense hardwoods like pear and elm. In many cases, the chips were barely a millimeter deep. Today, most chip carvers use basswood, a species that is less dense. Carvers, then, can make their chips as deep as they want.

Shallow chip carving is less time consuming than making the standard geometric chip. One reason is that, owing to the design, there are fewer chips to contend with. Generally, shallow chips are not side by side but are more widely spaced. Also, it does not work well to have vertical cuts from two different chips next to each other.

Figure 1 shows a three-sided chip in the shape of an elongated triangle. Dimension A equals the depth of the chip at its deepest end. The depth can vary depending on the density of the wood and the desired results. Angle B equals the angle or taper of the cut for sides 1 and 2. Note that the bottom of the chip is really at the front of the chip and not plumb center as with the geometric deep chip.

An economy of motion

When doing shallow chip carving with many chips, I cut all of the sides labeled 1 with my knife; then I cut all of the sides labeled 2. Last, I go back and cut all of the sides labeled 3.

The chess pieces and board by Barry McKenzie comprise 64 different rosettes. Note that the chess pieces are chip carved to their edges.

Three steps to carving a shallow chip

To chip carve a shallow chip, start with side 1, then do side 2. These are both vertical stop cuts with the tip of the blade touching the bottom of the chip. To cut side 3, make a flat, slicing motion that connects sides 1 and 2. The knife blade is turned flat on its side, parallel to the plane of the wood surface. For the chip to come out, the three cuts need to converge at the front of the chip down in the deep end. See **Figure 2**.

Side 1: Place the blade face vertically in the chip. The tip of the blade has to be at the bottom of the chip up in front at the deep end.

Side 2: Make the cut holding the blade face vertically, with the knife tip converging with the first cut up in front of the chip at the deep end.

Side 3: Done with the blade laid down flat. A slicing motion is used that stays within the cuts made for sides 1 and 2. The knife can be held in a grip that has the thumb beside the blade for a pull stroke or with the thumb behind the handle for a push stroke.

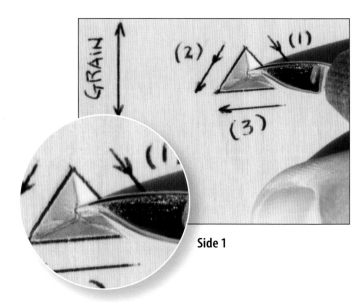
Side 1

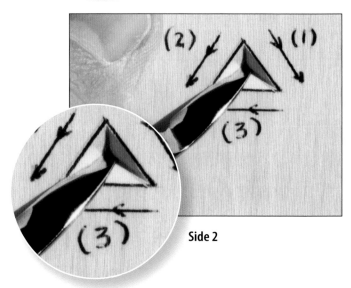
Side 2

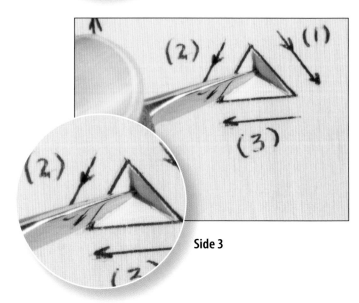
Side 3

Figure 1

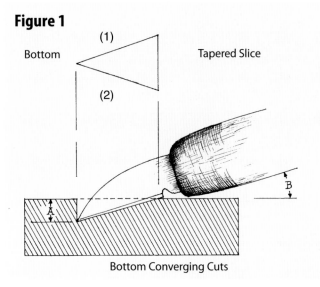

Bottom Converging Cuts

Figure 2

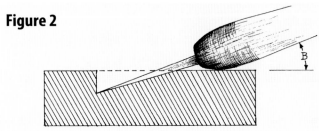

Sanding

The close up of the lid shows how chip carving through pre-stained basswood gives a pleasing contrast between the stain and the raw wood underneath.

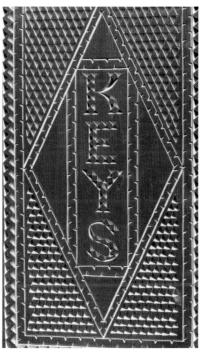

The lid of the key box was chip carved through stain by Barry McKenzie.

Sanding must be done before working the wood. After sanding, the carver can then draw on the wood or transfer the pattern. I recommend to students that they start with an ultra-smooth surface.

I use a sandpaper that does not have a gravel grit that comes off in the wood. Sandpaper with its grit fused on paper or cloth works best.

Some carvers sand away pencil lines and smudges after they complete the chip carving. I find that less of a problem on shallow chip carving than on carvings with geometric chips. It is too easy to flatten out the tops of the ridges between the chips on geometric deep chip carvings if sanding is done after the carving. Those ridges need to be left sharp. A soft eraser removes most lines. When finishing, rub off any pencil lines you may have missed when the finish is still wet.

The bentwood-style box with removable lid was made by L.A. "Chris" Christianson of Rochester, Minnesota. His work was a winner at the 1998 All Chip Carvers Show held in Lebanon, Missouri.

A view from above shows that "Chris" used two types of shallow chip carving.

Old-World-Style Chip Carving

TIP

On pages 12 to 19, I introduced the standard geometric deep chip and the shallow chip. Both are done with a chip carving knife that requires holding it in two different grips. The third style is called old-world-style chip carving. As the name suggests, it's been around for some time and is easily traced to the late 1800s.

Old world chip carving usually goes faster than geometric deep chip carving because there are fewer small chips to remove. Typically, the chips are longer and larger for the old-world-style chip. These take up more space, so there is less work involved.

MAKING VERTICAL STAB CUTS

I use a stabber knife with a skewed blade to make the vertical cuts. I cover the blade with masking tape to prevent the steel from reflecting the lines and causing confusion.

Vertical stab cuts can be executed efficiently if all are done at the same time. To reach the full width of the chip, I lever the knife down on the line, keeping the point at the bottom.

I drew the pattern in ink for this article. Light pencil lines are sufficient for a pattern.

Steps to carving an old-world-style chip

This example shows a four-sided chip in the form of a chevron. Dimension A (see **Figure 1**) equals the depth of the chip. The depth can vary depending on the carver's preference. Angle B equals the angle of the cut for sides 3 and 4. Sides 1 and 2 are vertical cuts. The bottom is the deepest part of the chip; it's also the point at which the four cuts converge.

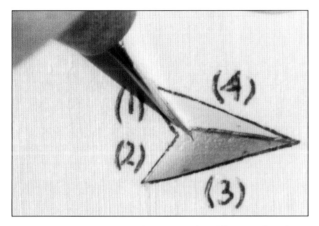

Start with the two vertical stop cuts for sides 1 and 2. These establish the bottom of the chip. The knife is held vertically.

Make the tapered cuts for sides 3 and 4. Use whichever knife position is more comfortable. This means that the thumb can be behind the handle or beside the blade. Make sure the two vertical cuts for sides 1 and 2 converge with the tapered cuts for sides 3 and 4. If all four cuts converge at the bottom, the chip will come out in one piece.

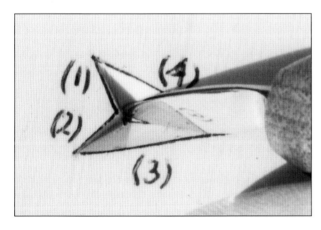

This is the reverse of removing the chip into the stop cut. Instead, cut from the deep end of the chip and out to the narrow end. Whichever method is used, make sure that all the cuts converge at the bottom.

Figure 1

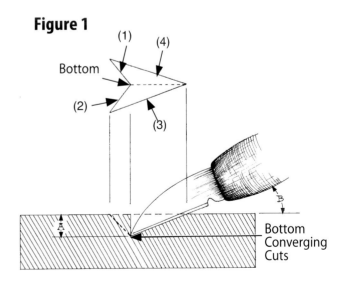

The box lid was made for a local church. The wood is a light butternut finished with three coats of Minwax Antique Oil Finish. The relief carving around the cross gives the illusion of it being raised above the surface. The old-world-style chips are in the cross and above and below the four-cornered chips in the margin patterns.

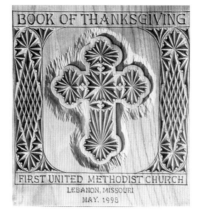

The butternut lid covers a box for wedding photos. The wood around the interlocking letters was textured with multiple small pin prick holes to give it a burnished look. The old-world-style chip patterns and a simple border strip were fitted around the letters. Plastic circle templates, French curves, and freehand drawing were used to fill in the pattern.

To make the design on the cross more interesting, the diamond shapes were notched to give them the look of small flower petals.

The chip carved cross shows an example of old world chip patterns filling an entire surface area and giving a celestial spiral appearance.

The box lid was an early project making use of old-world-style chip carving. Some patterns were outlined with thin lines, a chip carving style common in Sweden. This further defines the chip, giving the pattern the appearance of a mechanical pulley and wheel.

Free-form chip carving

Free-form chip carving is not as rigid in its execution as geometric deep chip carving (see page 12). But, while it uses the basic mechanics of knife holding, it also draws on the elements of artistry and free expression in how deeply the knife penetrates and at what angle it is held. Put another way, free-form chip carving is an extension of the carver's artistic talents after the mechanics of chip carving have been mastered. Some say it is "calligraphy with a knife."

Free-form chip carving works best with long, curving lines that are common to floral motifs. But figures can also be done with this style of chip carving where layout lines are guidelines that do not have to be followed precisely. These lines provide a track to follow while the carver changes the depth and angle of the knife. In contrast, geometric chip carving is executed with stab cuts directly into the wood to a uniform depth and angle of entry.

The second cut is being made on these free-form designs. The tip of the knife is tracking the bottom of the first cut. The angle of entry, width, and depth of the cut change constantly. For circular cuts, it helps to have a blade that has been stropped to a perfect cutting edge with the blade being as thin as possible.

Illustration 1

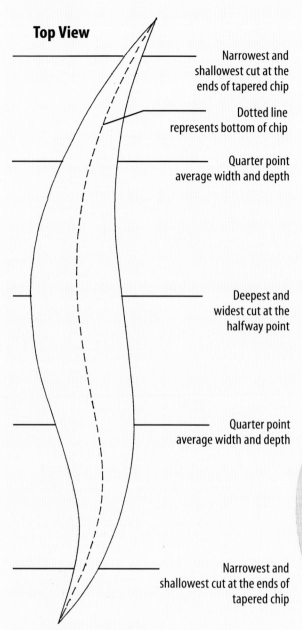

Top View

— Narrowest and shallowest cut at the ends of tapered chip

— Dotted line represents bottom of chip

— Quarter point average width and depth

— Deepest and widest cut at the halfway point

— Quarter point average width and depth

Narrowest and shallowest cut at the ends of tapered chip

End View (Cross Section)

Narrowest and shallowest cut

Deepest and widest cut

Quarter point average depth and width

45°

65° 55°

Bottom of deepest cut

When I teach this to my students, I explain that a stop cut, which is always the first cut, is the result of four techniques of execution. The first is the angle of the blade entry; the second is the width of the chip, the third is the depth; and the fourth is the bottom of the chip: the result of the previous three techniques.

With free-form chip carving, the cut is always changing in depth while the angle of the blade entry changes from one end of the cut to the other. **Illustration 1** shows how the depth of the cut changes while the angle of the blade entry varies from 45° to 65° as the knife is drawn through the wood from one end of the chip to the other. The second cut that removes the chip is tracked along the bottom groove of the stop cut and must mirror the execution techniques described above.

If the knife blade is undercutting the stop cut, residue will remain in the bottom of the chip. Overcutting will clean out the chip but will leave a deep and visible cut line in the bottom of the chip. To create a clean chip, the uniformity of depth must be controlled.

The flowers and butterflies on the heart-shaped box were designed and carved by Marion Turnipseed of Grove, Oklahoma.

The floral-design plate was carved by George Stadtlander of Mantua, Ohio.

The bold geometric chip carving on the rim is balanced with free-form chip carving in the bottom of this shallow butternut bowl chip carved by Barry McKenzie.

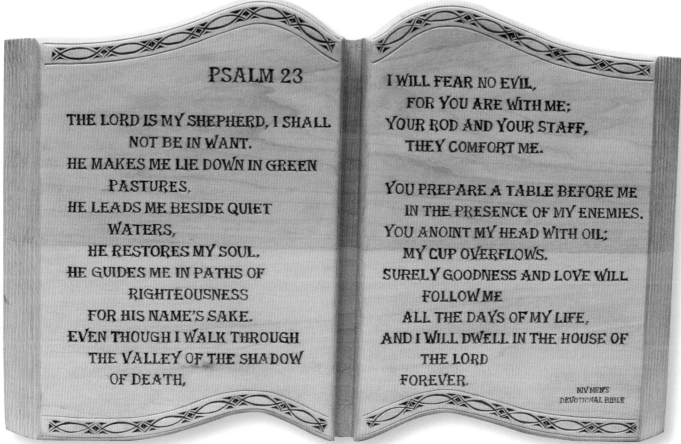

PSALM 23

THE LORD IS MY SHEPHERD, I SHALL
NOT BE IN WANT.
HE MAKES ME LIE DOWN IN GREEN
PASTURES,
HE LEADS ME BESIDE QUIET
WATERS,
HE RESTORES MY SOUL.
HE GUIDES ME IN PATHS OF
RIGHTEOUSNESS
FOR HIS NAME'S SAKE.
EVEN THOUGH I WALK THROUGH
THE VALLEY OF THE SHADOW
OF DEATH,

I WILL FEAR NO EVIL,
FOR YOU ARE WITH ME;
YOUR ROD AND YOUR STAFF,
THEY COMFORT ME.

YOU PREPARE A TABLE BEFORE ME
IN THE PRESENCE OF MY ENEMIES.
YOU ANOINT MY HEAD WITH OIL;
MY CUP OVERFLOWS.
SURELY GOODNESS AND LOVE WILL
FOLLOW ME
ALL THE DAYS OF MY LIFE,
AND I WILL DWELL IN THE HOUSE OF
THE LORD
FOREVER.

NIV MEN'S
DEVOTIONAL BIBLE

Lettering on the plaque that suggests an open Bible falls into the category of free-form chip carving. The piece was carved by Barry McKenzie.

Individual Styles

Chip carving has come a long way over the years with chip carvers being very inventive in their approaches to chip carving. This article introduces methods and styles that might be considered the signature work of chip carvers who are setting new trends for others to follow.

Jack Klein of South Haven, Minnesota incorporates the art of painting into his chip carving using two different methods. Method 1: The poinsettia was painted in after the free-form lines were chip carved out of the center of the plate. Method 2: The outside rim border, made up of leaf motifs, was actually chip carved through paint that was applied before the pattern was drawn in.

With a strong Norwegian heritage, L.A. "Chris" Christianson of Rochester, Minnesota, incorporates rosemaling from the Telemark District of Norway into his chip carving. Rosemaling is a very old style of Norwegian folk art that is decorative painting on wood. Characteristic of rosemaling are flowers done as scroll forms. Christianson's unpainted rosemaling-style scroll designs are executed with free-form cuts varying in depth and width. The bolder, free-form chips require successive cuts, with each cut making the chips deeper and wider. See **Figure 1**.

Jack Klein's plate brings together a painted, free-form chip carved pattern —the poinsettia— and chip carving through paint on the border.

"Chris" Christianson uses bold, deep, large, and small scroll chips in what he calls rosemaling design chip carving.

George Stadtlander of Mantua, Ohio, creates "Tramp Art." This style of chip carving is executed with repeated geometric type notches or cuts done on the edges of laminated wood. Tramp Art was popular in the United States between the Civil War and the Great Depression. A discarded cigar box or fruit crate in the hands of a craftsman could be transformed into an intricately chip carved picture frame, box or chest. When itinerant carvers made a piece, it was often used as barter for food or lodging.

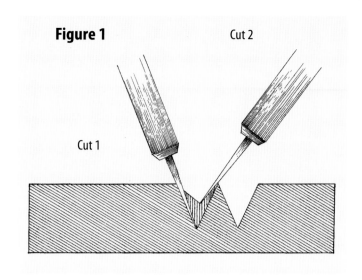

Figure 1

Cut 2

Cut 1

Cut 1 removes a significantly large portion of the wood in the scroll cut. Cut 2 removes the remainder of the wood down to the bottom of the chip. This is a useful technique when chip carving free-form patterns.

George Stadtlander's Tramp Art, geometric in design, uses laminated pieces of wood to create a box.

Russ Hewitt of Lebanon, Missouri, calls his style of chip carving "Gouge Chip" because he uses gouges instead of a knife to remove the chips. In Sweden, removing chips with gouges, skewer knives or chisels is more commonly done than in North America. Those who feel that their chip carving days are numbered might want to look into this alternate style. See **Figure 2**.

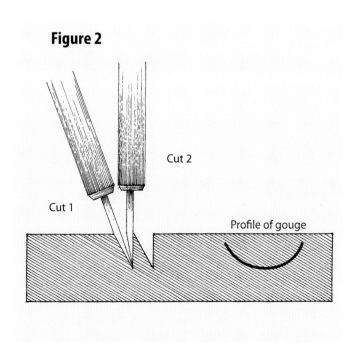

Figure 2

Cut 2

Cut 1

Profile of gouge

Gouge sweeps in gouge chip carving range from no. 3 to no. 11, with widths from 1/16" to 9/16". Cut 1 creates a vertical stop cut from the gouge, setting up chip removal in the next cut. In Cut 2, the gouge enters at an angle and wood is removed as it would be with a chip carving knife.

Russ Hewitt's gouge chip carving is one of the ultimate forms of nontraditional chip carving because a gouge replaces a knife to remove wood.

Decorations, Christmas Ornaments & More

A fun approach to learning chip carving comes with practicing on small, handheld decorations. The range of pieces that can be chip carved is limited only by your imagination. And even if the results are less than perfect, the decorations will still brighten up a tree, window, or mantel, or make great gifts to those who are special.

What makes decorations especially interesting is piercing them. This means that the piece is cut through with a chip carving knife so that light or a solid background can show through. I find that ³⁄₃₂"-thick basswood works very well for the pierced, chip-carved decorations I make. The wood holds up amazingly well no matter how narrow the wood becomes between the chips.

A stylized angel made by Cynthia Miles of Gardendale, Texas, was the first-place winner in the 1997 Chip Carved Ornament Contest sponsored by the "Chip Carvers Newsletter."

The hummingbird by Cindy Neill of Medford, New York took fourth place.

The third-place winner was Dale Johnson of Madison, Wisconsin. The ornament can be worn as a pendant.

This pierced ornament is a "sandwich" composed of three discs of wood. Most of the center disc has been removed. For a novel effect, insert a small round mirror into the center. Colored cellophane or foil can also be inserted into the center of the middle disc for a stained glass appearance.

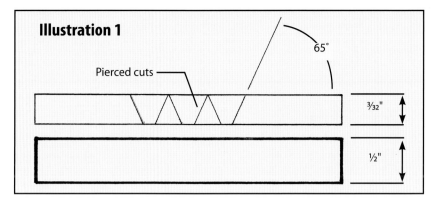

Illustration 1

Pierced cuts

65°

3/32"

1/2"

The 3"-diameter decoration is made from three pieces of wood sandwiched together. The front piece has pierced lettering. The center was drilled out with a Forstner bit, and a round plug was inserted to offer a contrast in the design. The Christmas tree hanger for the decoration was shaped using a carving knife.

While thin basswood is fairly easy to pierce, it is necessary to have a backing board of scrap wood or plywood (see **Illustration 1**). A board ½" thick or more will suffice to protect the hand holding the decoration. Once the pattern is established, the angle of the blade entry needs to be steep and deep if it is to penetrate through the wood in one pass. I recommend having the blade enter at about 65°. If you want to enlarge the pierced chip, you can always carve away some of the wood from the back of the cut with the knife.

The variety of pierced ornaments is nearly limitless. In fact, once an ornament is cut through, it can be further shaped with traditional carving tools, painted, or backed with colored paper or foil to give it the appearance of a stained glass decoration. Whatever you decide, don't forget to sign the ornament with name and date. It won't take that many years before your work will become a treasured collectible.

These scrolls that bear spiritual messages are approximately 3" tall. Before cutting the wood to shape, first type the message on a piece of paper to fit a small rectangular format. Then, using transfer paper, transfer it to an oversized piece of wood, which is easier to work with. Once the letters are chip carved, cut away the excess wood.

The chip carved ornament by Mark Stryker of Jersey Shore, Pennsylvania, took second place in the 1997 Chip Carved Ornament Contest.

The pierced star was done from butternut. The bevels on the points were shaped using a carving knife.

Bible ornaments measure 1½" tall, ¾" wide, and ½" thick. The ornament is made from four pieces of wood sandwiched together.

Holiday Projects

These holiday project are easy to complete and great for practicing the different types of chips. They also make excellent gifts for the special people in your life. Once you master the basics, you'll be able to quickly make these designs and many more of your own ideas and variations.

Geometric Ornaments,
by Roger Strautman, page 57.

Snowflake Ornament

by Roger Nancoz, Photography by Roger Schroeder

Follow this step-by-step procedure to create a beautiful snowflake chip carving. After completing this project, you will have a solid foundation in sharpening a chip-carving knife, preparing wood for carving, and making actual chip cuts.

1

Have your tools and materials at hand. The tools and materials of chip carving range from knives to wood to pattern to sharpening compound.

Size to fit blank of choice

Sharpening your knife

2

Prepare to sharpen. I scrape my honing compound onto a block of wood. The solid surface of the wood keeps the point of the knife sharper than leather does.

3 **Sharpen the knife at a 10° angle.** Sharpening is essential. It's the only way to get clean cuts. The knife is almost held flat to the wood surface.

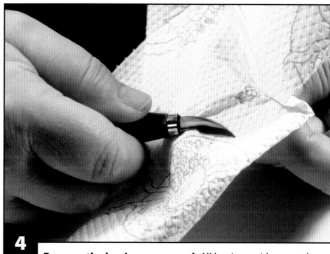

4 **Remove the honing compound.** All honing residue must be removed from the knife or it gets into the wood.

Attaching the pattern

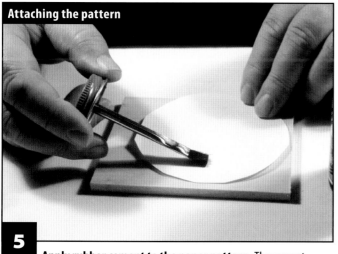

5 **Apply rubber cement to the paper pattern.** The cement makes for easy paper removal. Be sure to work in a well ventilated room. Coat the wood with rubber cement. This is only after the wood has been sanded and sealed with lacquer. The sealer reduces grain tearout.

Making a three-sided chip

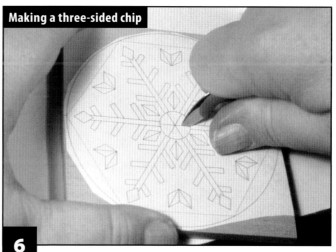

6 **Make the first cut in position one.** The way I hold the knife is called position one in chip carving. Before I carve, I make sure my thumbnail is well manicured or covered with tape. If not, the nail will mark the wood, even with the pattern attached. Carefully align the pattern. Keep the design flowing with the grain. Notice that I keep the waste wood to a minimum.

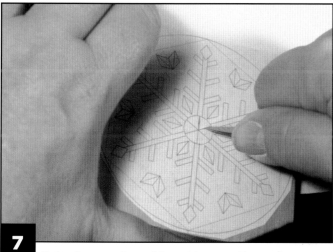

7 **Make the second cut with position two.** The number two position is a backhand cut. Which stroke I use depends on grain direction and position of the wood.

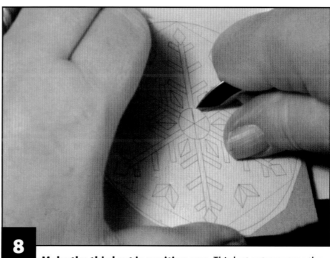

8 **Make the third cut in position one.** This last cut prepares the chip for removal.

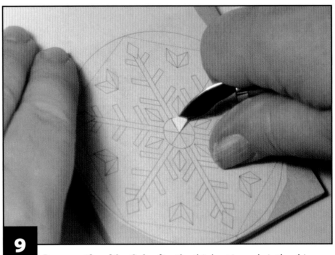

9 **Remove the chip.** Only after the third cut is made is the chip loose. A thin knife in chip carving is essential. Too much wood is displaced with a thick blade and the wooden ridge will break out.

10 **Finish carving the center rosette.** After finishing the center rosette of six triangular chips, I clean the area with a gummy eraser to remove paper, rubber cement, and dirt.

Making a four-sided chip

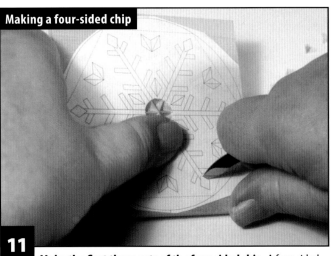

11 **Make the first three cuts of the four-sided chip.** A four-sided chip is more advanced. Imagine the point of the knife is going directly to the middle of the chip. If the angles are correct, the knife will go to the center. For this kind of chip, I practice on scrap wood.

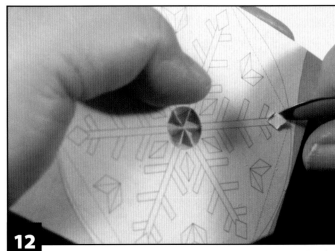

12 **Remove the chip with the last cut.** I finish the fourth side of the chip and release it.

Making a straight chip

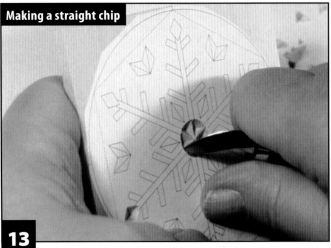

13 **Make a stop cut.** I start on the spoke of the snowflake at the center rosette at about a 65° angle to the surface. The cut forms a ridge between the spoke and the rosette.

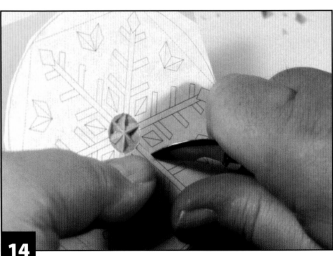

14 **Cut the first side.** Here, I use the number one position going down one side of the spoke.

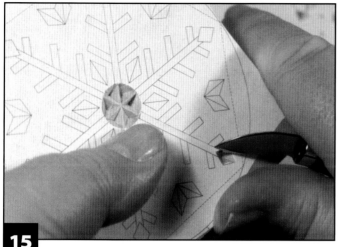

15 **Try to avoid tearout.** When I reach the end of the spoke, rather than drag the knife into the four-sided chip, I tilt the knife downward. This reduces the possibility of tearing out wood, especially if I am not going with the grain.

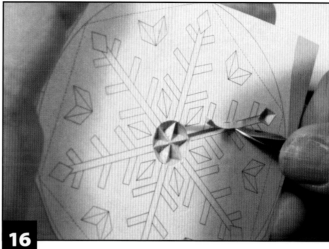

16 **Cut the second side.** Here I use the number two position. When I see the chip peel out, I know I have carved it properly.

17 **Check your progress.** Notice how the chip has been cleanly removed from the spoke.

Cutting the branches

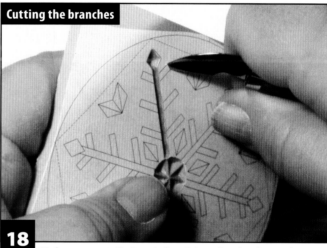

18 **Make stop cuts.** Each spoke has six branches. I make simple stop cuts to begin removal. To save time, instead of moving the wood around and doing the branches individually, I do them in sequence, making a stop cut on all of them. Economizing motion picks up the pace.

19 **Cut the first side.** One way to do a branch is to start from the stop cut at the end of the branch and carve into the spoke.

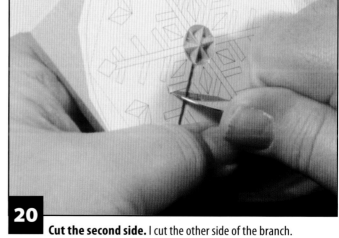

20 **Cut the second side.** I cut the other side of the branch.

21 **Clean the cut.** After the chip is released, I use an old toothbrush to remove fuzzy grain.

Cutting another branch

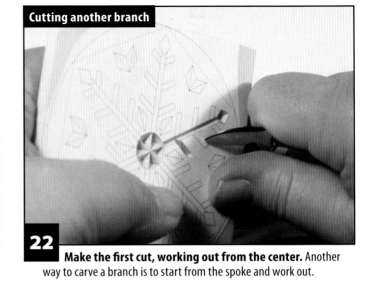

22 **Make the first cut, working out from the center.** Another way to carve a branch is to start from the spoke and work out.

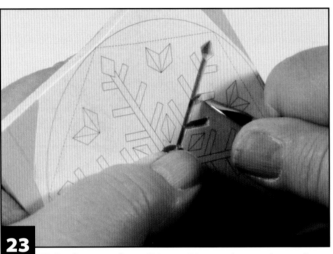

23 **Make the second cut.** Using position number two, I carve the other side of the branch.

Cutting back-to-back triangles

24 **Cut one side of the ridge.** These triangles have a common ridge that is perpendicular to the grain. First, make a stop cut to cut away the left-hand chip from the center ridge. To reduce breakout, I always cut the ridges of butting chips first .

25 **Cut the other side.** Here, I do the other side of the ridge, performing the same cut to prevent fracturing the wood.

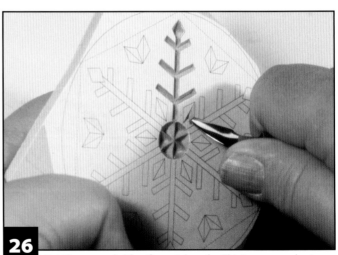

26 **Cut the second side of one triangle.** This is my second cut in the sequence to carve the diamonds. The chip starts to peel out because of the grain.

27 **Make the final cut.** The ease with which the chip pops out means I made clean cuts all around.

28 **Cut the other triangle.** I carve the other side of the adjacent triangles.

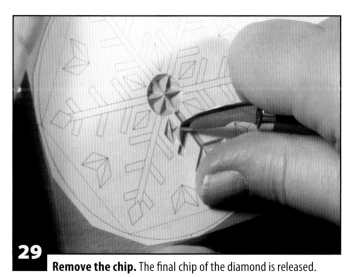

29 **Remove the chip.** The final chip of the diamond is released.

Cutting flying diamonds

30 **Cut around the fragile ridge.** This cut is tricky because of the merging lines in the middle of what I call "flying diamonds." Where the lines merge, there is a tendency for the wood to break out. I take each chip out without carving its fragile point.

31 **Cut the ridge.** All four triangles have been cut on the flying diamonds, but notice that the paper is still present in the merging lines. I then carefully slice out the wood under the paper.

32 **Complete the carving and finish.** All major cuts have been made on the piece on the right. The board on the left shows the finished carving. I use my band saw and a 1" belt sander to finish the edge. Then, I remove the paper, sand, and seal the wood.

Tree Ornaments

By Barry McKenzie

The chip carved tree ornament is a project that helped a lot of carvers I know learn their basic cuts. In the seven steps that follow, I provide easy-to-follow techniques that will produce an ornament sure to delight all who see it.

▲ **Step 1: Make it bright.** Choose a piece of wood ¼" thick. I recommend basswood, cedar, poplar, aspen, or another soft wood. Cut out the outline on a band saw or scroll saw or use a coping saw. If necessary, sand rough edges with medium-grit sandpaper.

Chip carved ornaments stand out when color is applied. Use the paint at full strength and apply it directly to the wood with a small bristle brush. Wait at least a half hour for the paint to set up before tracing the pattern. Check the blade's cutting edge frequently to make sure that it is not getting dull. Avoid using any metallic paint because the metal particles will literally eat away the cutting edge.

▲ **Step 2: Transfer the pattern.** When using darkly painted wood, white transfer paper works best for putting the pattern onto the cutout. It's a better choice than carbon paper because lines are easily erased, even after the chips are carved. With the transfer paper under the pattern, draw over the lines with a rounded-tip hard lead pencil, a fine-tip ballpoint pen, or a stylus. Do not press down so hard that you dent the painted wood.

Step 3: Keep it safe. Chip carving can be practiced on a flat work surface, but you'll find it easier to accomplish if one hand holds the work and the other grips the knife. A leather or cut-resistant glove is a wise investment. Try also using a backing piece of wood between the ornament and your hand. Try a piece of ¼"-thick plywood or hardwood cut to the shape of the ornament.

Step 6: Make the third cut. In this step, you are duplicating the angle of entry made in Steps 4 and 5. With experience, you will feel the blade; you are duplicating the angle of entry made in Steps 4 and 5. You will feel the blade bottoming out and actually converging with the bottom of the cut made in Step 4 and the cut executed in Step 5. The goal is to make each chip uniform at its bottom so the three cuts converge at one point. If the chip has to be pried out, the cuts have not met uniformly.

▲ **Step 4: Make a stop cut.** The first stab of the blade is called a stop cut, an operation that performs three functions: it establishes the angle of the blade entry; it cuts to the width of the chip for uniformity of depth; and it determines the bottom of the chip where the tip of the blade stops. Notice in the picture how the blade is in the wood to the width of the chip. This ensures the uniformity of depth for each chip.

Make an entry angle of about 45°, using the grip shown in the photo. Keep in mind that the depth of a cut measures out very close to the width of a chip. Also be aware that the steeper you make the blade's entry angle, the deeper the cut is going to be. Obviously, the depth of the cut should never exceed the thickness of the wood.

Step 5: Make the second cut. The second cut goes in at the same angle of entry as the stop cut made in Step 4.

Size to fit blank of choice

▲ **Step 7: Fix an undercut.** It's inevitable that the knife makes undercuts, meaning that one cut goes beneath another. The result is a ridge of wood that lifts up in the bottom of the chip. Don't discard your project or attempt to clean out the existing cuts. Instead, press down on the raised portion of wood with the tip of a bamboo chopstick or skewer stick. You might be tempted to use the back of the chip carving knife, but steel tends to damage the wood.

Leaf Ornaments

By Barry McKenzie

Hand carve ornaments for everyone on your list with these elegant leaf designs.

Ornaments are a great way to practice your chip carving skills. They are small enough to be held in one hand, so you can carve them almost anywhere. If your ornament comes out a little rough, well, primitive ornaments are still popular.

In my study of old-world-style chip carving in Sweden, Italy, and the Friesland area of Holland, the leaf design was used as filler in the chip carved pattern. I took that design and used it as the primary design on these ornaments.

After finishing a few and mastering the hand positions, you'll be able to complete a whole set in no time.

A WORD ON SAFETY **TIP**

Because the wood used for ornaments may only be ¼" thick, you should use a reinforcing piece of scrap wood as a backing when holding the ornament and chip carving. Otherwise, the knife may go the whole way through the ornament into your skin.

Materials & Tools

Materials:
- ¼" x 3¼" x 4¼" oval basswood blank or blank of choice
- Sandpaper, 220 grit
- Sealing finish
- Stain (optional)
- Nail or carvers punch
- Round eye punch (optional)

Tools:
- Chip carving knife

| LEAF 1 | LEAF 2 | LEAF 3 | LEAF 4 | LEAF 5 | LEAF 6 | LEAF 7 |

It's easy to change the shape and size of the leaf design once you are familiar with the techniques. All seven of these leaves were carved using the same basic procedure.

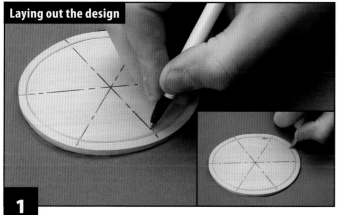

1   **Trace or draw the pattern onto the wood.** Start by drawing a line around the outside. Make a cut following this line around the perimeter of the ornament. Hold your knife at a 65° angle, and make the cut toward the line around the perimeter of the ornament. Cut into the line from the other side to meet the first cut, again holding your knife at a 65° angle to release the chip. I also drew in a few reference lines to help me line up the pattern.

2   **Center the leaf design inside your line cut.** Use your reference lines as a guide. Use graphite paper under the pattern to trace the basic leaf design. Use a pen to fill in any places the graphite paper missed.

Cutting the design

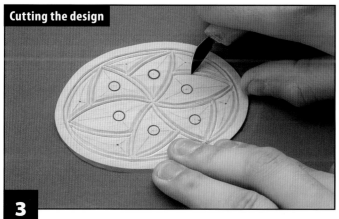

3   **Make line cuts around the perimeter of each leaf.** Again, hold your knife at a 65° angle. Cut toward the line with your first cut. Cut in at a 65° angle from the opposite direction to release the chip. You want to leave a thin, raised division to separate the leaves. Draw in the circles, and sketch the lines of your next cut.

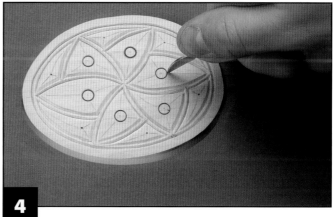

4   **Cut out three triangular chips from each leaf.** Make a circle cut around the center circle. Alternatively, use a circle punch to make a perfect circle. Then, make a cut down the center of each leaf section, holding your knife at a 90° angle. Hold your knife nearly parallel to the wood (at less than a 45° angle), and cut in toward the center. Work your way around the entire leaf section that way. You want to scoop out the center of each leaf section.

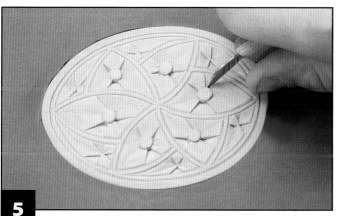

5   **Define the leaves.** Hold your knife at a 90° angle and make two shallow cuts by pressing the tip of your knife into the center of the each leaf section. Then hold your knife almost parallel to the board, and take a chip out from between these two cuts. Do this three times on each leaf section and in each section between the tips of the leaves.

6   **Detail the leaves.** Use very small line cuts to add a center vein and small V-shaped cuts to add the side details to each leaf. Use a carver's punch or a small nail to add texture to the leaf center circles and background. Give the carving a light sanding with 220-grit sandpaper to remove any pencil lines. Apply a sealing finish and stain as desired.

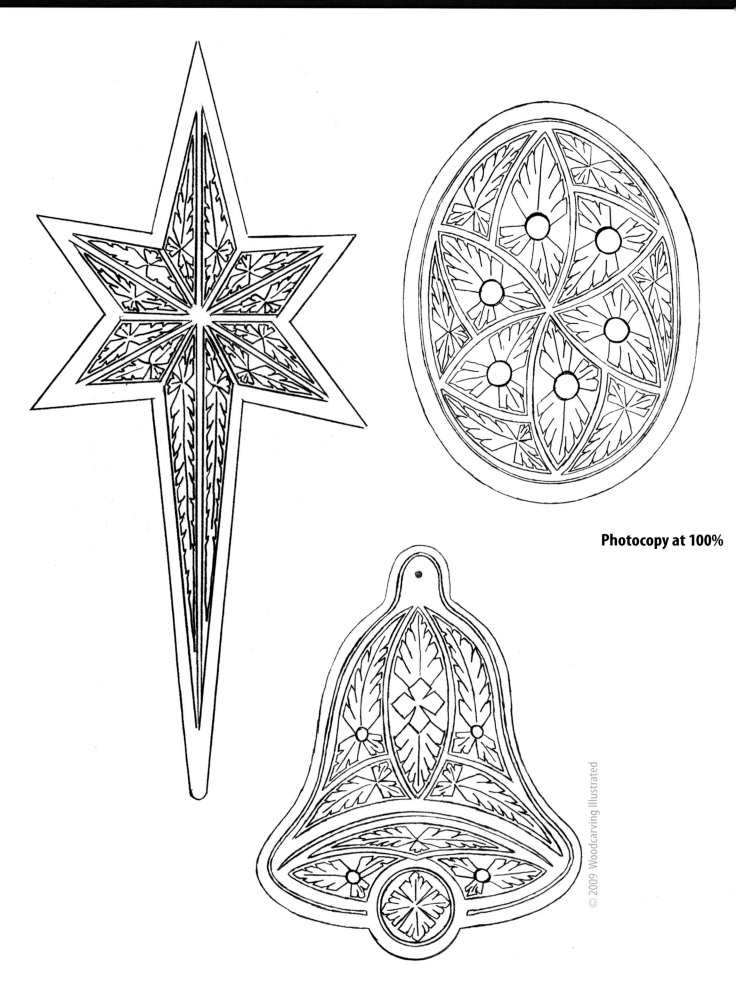

Photocopy at 100%

© 2009 Woodcarving Illustrated

Star Tree Topper

By Roger Strautman

Chip carving is my passion. I'm always looking for creative new ideas. My latest inspiration came from a star on a banner in our church. I designed this chip carved Christmas tree star based on the star on the banner. I use basswood for the project and bleach the wood before carving. Carving through the bleached wood exposes the unbleached wood in the chip cavities, which provides contrast and highlights the design.

You can make the star two ways. If you are not comfortable cutting compound angles, create the star as a flat design. You can create a flat star with simple miter cuts or by cutting the perimeter of the star from a single piece of wood. A star made from a single piece of wood will be more fragile than one built from mitered panels.

To create the 3-D star featured in this article, you will need to make compound miter cuts. The miter cut is made at an angle across the face of the board. This miter cut is combined with a beveled cut, which is made by tilting the blade on an angle. The miter and bevel cuts are made simultaneously.

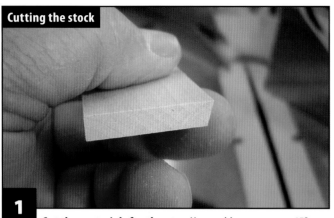

1 **Cut the materials for the star.** Use a table saw to cut a 15° bevel on one long side of all four ¼" x 1¼" x 24" basswood blanks. Create a gluing jig to make it easier to glue the blanks together. To make the jig, nail two strips of scrap wood 2⁷⁄₁₆" apart on a flat sheet of scrap wood. These strips will hold the blanks together at the proper angle.

2 **Glue the strips together.** Apply glue to the beveled side of two strips. Align these strips on the gluing jig with the angled sides against each other. Position a clamp at the joint on both ends and apply a little pressure. Use the same method to glue the other two strips together. After the glue dries, sand both sides of the strips with 220-grit sandpaper.

3 **Make the first compound cut.** Square all four ends of the glued stock. Tilt the blade of the compound miter saw to 3° and set the saw to cut a 45° miter. Place the square end of the stock against the fence and position the stock so the miter cut ends at the glue joint in the stock. Clamp a piece of scrap wood on the saw table against the side of the blank to act as a second fence. Make this cut on all four ends of the blanks.

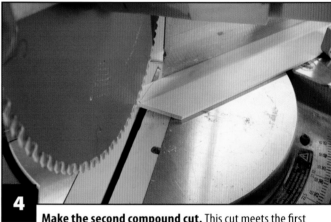

4 **Make the second compound cut.** This cut meets the first cut, creating a point. The four points will form the center of the star. Do not change the settings on the saw. Remove the scrap wood fence. Turn the glued stock 90° and position it against the fence on the miter saw table. Line the stock up so the miter cut starts at the point where the first cut ended.

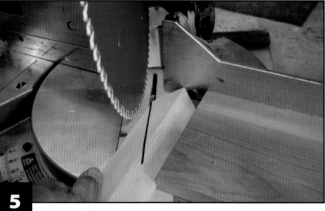

5 **Make the first perimeter cut.** Leave the blade tilted at the same angle and set the saw to cut a 22½° miter. Position the stock on the saw table with the point you just created against the fence. Line up the blank so the cut runs from the end of the first miter to the center joint. Clamp a piece of scrap wood on the miter saw table as a temporary fence. Only make this cut on three ends.

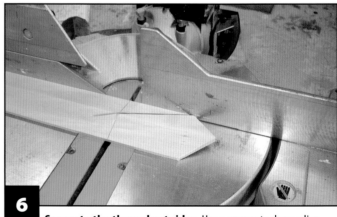

6 **Separate the three short sides.** Use a square to draw a line across the strip at the point where the cut made in Step 5 intersects with the centerline of the blanks. Square the blade and miter on the miter saw to make this cut or use a table saw. Cut the three sections free from the strips of glued stock. These will become the three short points on the star.

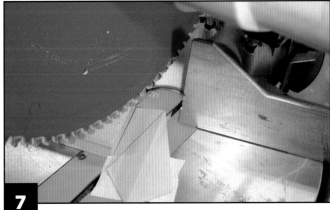

7 **Make the second perimeter cut.** With the blade tilted to 3° and the saw set to cut a 22½° miter, place the square end against the saw fence. Use scrap wood for a second fence. Because there is no way to safely hold the small stock, secure the section to the saw table with double-sided carpet tape. Complete the cut to finish forming the three short star points.

8 **Cut the long point of the star.** Keep the blade tilted at the same angle, but set the saw to cut a 12° miter. Use the method explained in Steps 5 through 7 to cut the long point. Assemble the star. Apply wood glue to two adjacent sides and hold them together for a few minutes until the glue grabs. Attach the other two points, using the same technique.

Embellishing the surface

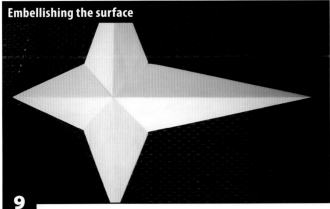

9 **Bleach the wood.** Allow the glue to dry overnight. Apply wood bleach to both sides of the basswood to turn the wood bright white. Apply a light coat of lacquer to both sides of the star to keep it clean while you carve and make it easier to remove the pencil lines when you are finished.

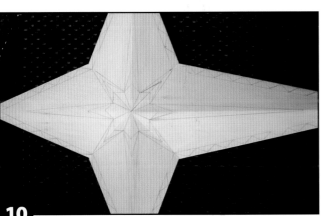

10 **Transfer the pattern to the star.** Wash your hands first. The oils in your skin may discolor the wood. Use the pattern provided or create your own design. Use graphite paper to trace the pattern on both sides of the star or draw the pattern with a 5mm mechanical pencil and a flexible ruler.

11 **Carve the center design.** Pick a spot on the convex side and carve the chips in a counterclockwise direction. Make the first cut next to the last chip to keep from losing the ridge between the chips. Keep the blade at a consistent angle and carve the chips so the cuts intersect in the center.

Completing the carving

12 **Carve the long chips.** Work out from the center, again moving in a counterclockwise direction. Use the same technique explained in Step 11 and complete the convex side. Repeat Steps 11 and 12 on the concave side. Be careful not to carve the entire way through the star.

13 **Carve the flat border.** The chips on the border are fragile. Make a running cut along the line parallel to the edge. Work one star point at a time. Cut the first side of the triangle on all the chips along one star point. Go back and cut the second side of the triangle to free the chip. Repeat on the opposite side of the star.

14 **Shape the edge of the star.** Begin to remove the wood between the chips cut in Step 13 by making a stop cut in the middle of the triangle to control the cut. Cut in from both sides toward the stop cut to free the chip. Repeat this step on both sides of the star. Clean up any rough chips and erase any remaining pencil marks.

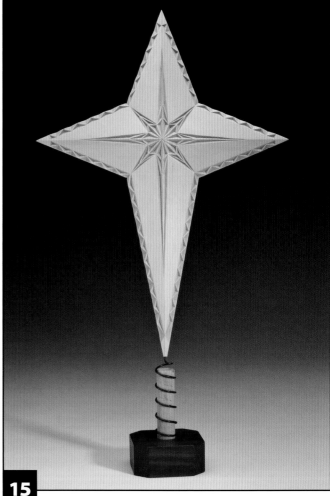

15 **Finish the star.** Seal both sides of the star with eight to ten light coats of lacquer. Drill a small hole in the base of the star. Straighten one end of a large spring and glue the straightened end in the hole. The spring will hold the star in place on the tree. Create a year-round display by gluing a ½"-diameter dowel into a hardwood base.

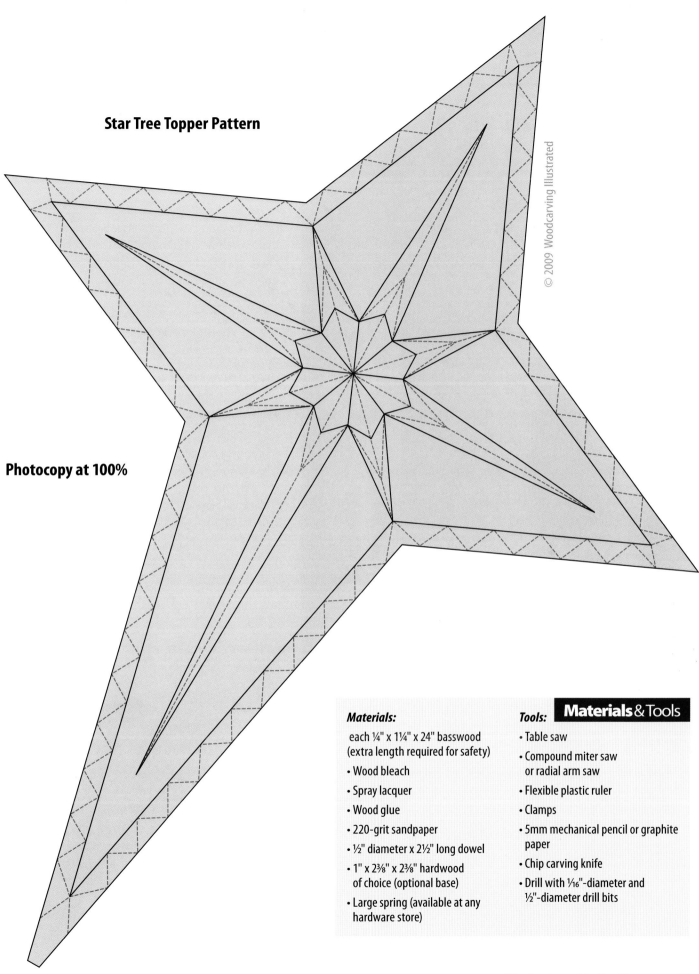

Star Tree Topper Pattern

Photocopy at 100%

© 2009 Woodcarving Illustrated

Materials &Tools

Materials:
each ¼" x 1¼" x 24" basswood (extra length required for safety)
- Wood bleach
- Spray lacquer
- Wood glue
- 220-grit sandpaper
- ½" diameter x 2½" long dowel
- 1" x 2⅜" x 2⅜" hardwood of choice (optional base)
- Large spring (available at any hardware store)

Tools:
- Table saw
- Compound miter saw or radial arm saw
- Flexible plastic ruler
- Clamps
- 5mm mechanical pencil or graphite paper
- Chip carving knife
- Drill with ¹⁄₁₆"-diameter and ½"-diameter drill bits

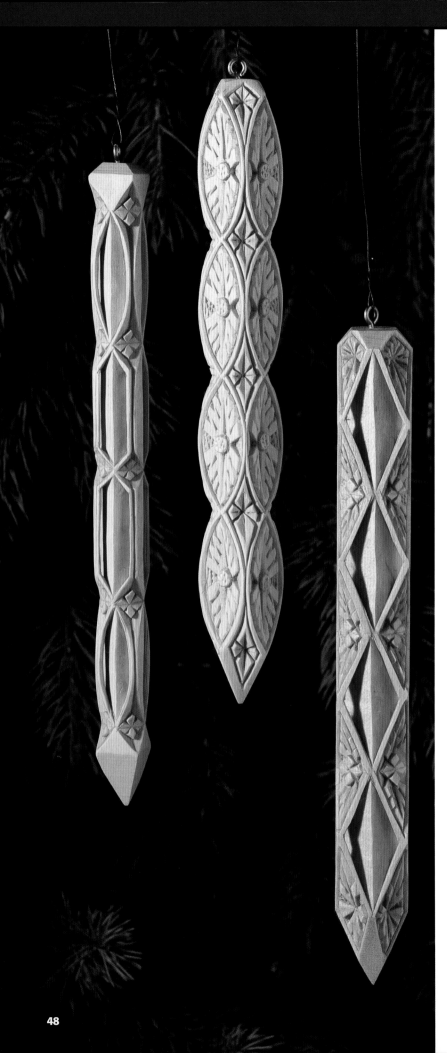

Delicate Icicle Ornaments

By Barry McKenzie

These ornaments combine old-world-style chip carving and tramp-art carving. Tramp-art or hobo-style carving incorporates the edge of the wood into the design.

Piercing on the edges of the icicles, where the patterns line up, creates a unique and delicate-looking ornament. All that's required is a block of wood and a chip carving knife.

After carving, attach a small screw eye to the top. This allows you to hang the ornaments for display and also provides something to hold on to when applying the finish. Apply just enough finish to dampen the surface. Then, add three more coats of finish, applying more finish and wetting the wood more each time to seal the wood around the cuts. The final coat should flood down in the chips. This way I get crisper, cleaner-looking cuts in all my chip carving.

Materials & Tools

Materials:
- Icicle blank (size the blank to match your skill level)
- Finish of choice (I use Danish oil or tung oil)
- Small screw eye

Tools:
- Chip carving knife of choice
- Graphite paper (to trace pattern)
- Brushes to apply finish

Icicle ornament patterns

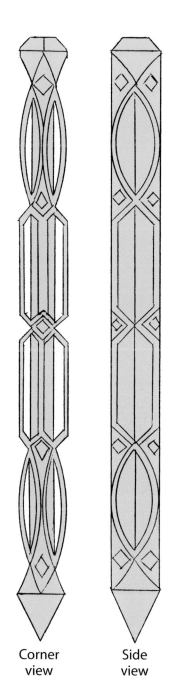

Corner
view

Side
view

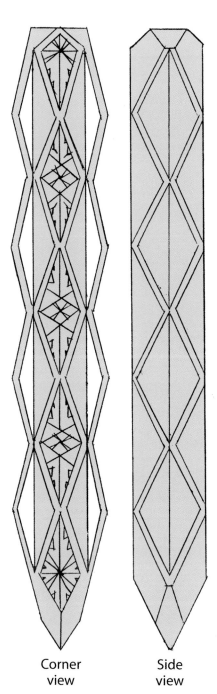

Corner
view

Side
view

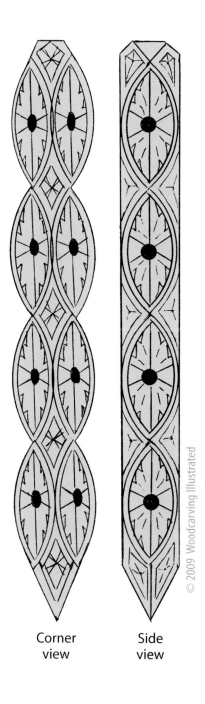

Corner
view

Side
view

Size the blank to match your skill level

Honeycomb Ornaments

By Linda Tudor

I love the look of delicate paper honeycomb decorations, but wanted ornaments that would be more durable. With these designs, I emphasized feeling rather than replication. Chip carving creates the same honeycomb effect and the tassels complete the Victorian-era feel.

It is difficult to accurately trace a pattern onto a round blank, so you'll probably want to draw the designs right on the wood. Since these designs represent intricately glued and folded paper, slight inaccuracies in the shape and size of the carved diamonds add to their character.

Start with commercially available basswood shapes or carve your own eggs and spheres from blocks of basswood. To carve a sphere, start with a square block. Use a compass to draw a circle the same size on all six sides of the block. Using a bench knife, carve the square into a sphere using these lines as a guide. Use a similar method to create blanks for the egg shape or ovals that dangle from the bottom of the ornaments. The procedure for drawing the honeycomb design is identical for all of the shapes.

Draw the Patterns

Step 1: Draw a horizontal line around the blank. For the sphere, measure the distance from the top of the ornament to the bottom and divide this dimension by two. Use a compass to draw a centerline around the circumference of the blank. The horizontal line for the egg shape is drawn three-fifths of the way down from the ornament's top.

Step 2: Determine the circumference of the blank. Wrap a piece of string or ribbon around the blank at the horizontal line. Mark the string where it crosses the end. Remove the string from the blank and measure the distance from the end to the mark. This dimension is the circumference of the blank.

Step 3: Divide the main ornament into 16 equal sections. Divide the circumference by 16. Use this measurement to mark the 16 segments along the horizontal line. Use a flexible ruler to draw vertical lines from the marks on the horizontal line to either end of the ornament. These vertical lines represent the center of the diamond-shaped chips along the horizontal line. The smaller dangling shapes are divided into eight equal sections.

Step 4: Draw in the diamonds. Draw the first ring of diamonds along the horizontal line. The top and bottom points of the diamonds line up with the vertical lines. Work your way to both ends using the first row of diamonds and the vertical lines as a guide. The diamonds narrow as you approach the top and bottom of the ornament.

Carve and Paint the Ornaments

Step 5: Carve the diamonds. The center of the diamond is the deepest point of the chip. Cut in at an angle on all four lines of the diamond. Angle the knife so all of the cuts intersect at the center of the chip. As the diamonds narrow, the chips become shallower. Leave an uncarved border approximately $1/16$" thick between the diamonds.

Step 6: Paint the ornaments. Thin acrylic paint to create a wash and make sure to get down into the center of each diamond. Apply as many coats as necessary to get the shade desired.

Step 7: Finish the ornaments. I make my own eyelets with 24-gauge silver wire. Drill a small hole with a drill bit slightly larger than the diameter of the wire. Cut a piece of wire and bend it to shape around the end of a paintbrush. Glue the eyelets into the holes with cyanoacrylate (CA) glue. Use the same method to attach the dangling ovals on the bottom. I crocheted the hanging cords and created a tassel out of #2 nylon crochet thread. Tassels are available at most craft supply stores.

Materials & Tools

Materials:
- 1¾" x 1¾" basswood stock (sphere-shaped ornament)
- 2½" x 2" basswood stock (egg-shaped ornament)
- ½" x1½" basswood stock (oval dangler for egg shape)
- ½" x 3" basswood stock (oval dangler for sphere shape)
- #2 nylon crochet thread (tassel and hanging cord)
- 24-gauge silver wire

- Acrylic paint of choice
- Cyanoacrylate (CA) glue

Tools:
- Bench knife
- Chip carving knife
- Round-nose pliers & wire cutter
- Drill and bit slightly larger than the diameter of the wire
- #12 crochet hook to chain stitch hanging cord (optional)

Delicate Pierced Ornaments

By Barry McKenzie

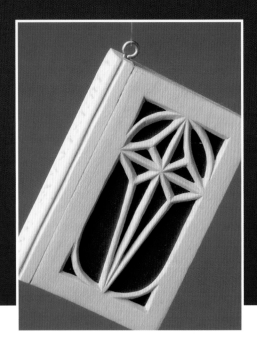

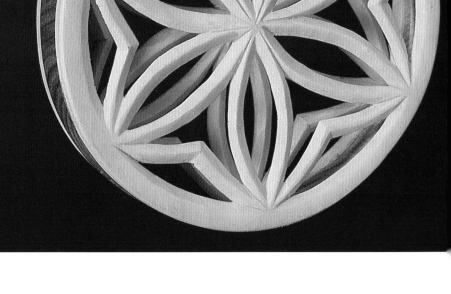

Chip carving is a traditional art form typically used as an embellishment. This creative project allows chip carving to take center stage. By cutting the whole way through the wood, you produce an elegant design ideal for Christmas ornaments. The technique uses basic chip carving skills, and with a little practice, you'll have a tree full of ornaments in no time.

Pierced, chip carved designs are typically carved in thin basswood. The fretwork or lace design is first carved on the front. Then, the ornament is flipped over and carved from the back to produce attractive negative space that highlights the design.

Many conventional chip carving patterns can be converted to pierced chip carving patterns. As long as the carved areas of the pattern are bordered by interconnected wood, they can be carved with the piercing technique. It does take a bit of practice to master these techniques, so I recommend experimenting with scrap wood first. Practice "applied pressure," where you apply just enough pressure to

cut through the wood without pressing hard enough to split the thin wood. Aggressive or heavy-handed carving tends to split the wood.

To get started, cut all three blanks oversized. The blanks will be sanded to the final dimensions when finished. The patterns are drawn for regular-size ornaments, but you may want to enlarge them and carve bigger ornaments until you are comfortable with the technique. Draw the final diameter on the blank. Transfer the rest of the pattern to the blank. I draw the design right on the blank with a circle template and mechanical pencil, but you can transfer the design to the blank with carbon paper.

I use a backing board when I am chip carving a small project. The backing board gives me a firm surface to cut into. When I'm carving a delicate design using the applied pressure technique, the backing board makes it much easier to control the chip carving knife. It also prevents me from cutting through the ornament into my hand. For additional protection, you can wear a carving glove.

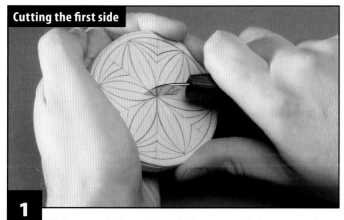

Cutting the first side

1 **Make a vertical cut through the center of the areas to be removed.** Cut at least halfway through. This relief cut keeps the wood from splitting when you carve the other elements.

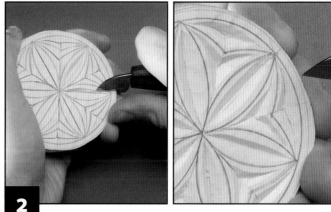

2 **Make the first cuts to define the elements.** Remove a small amount of wood on either side of the front relief cut. Make these cuts on all of the elements. This is a narrow but deep cut.

3 **Cut through the blank.** Continue to make shaving cuts on the left and right side of the cuts you made in Step 2 until you reach the pattern lines. At this point the center of the elements should be hollow. The ornament is about 60% complete.

Cutting the second side

4 **Draw the pattern on the other side of the blank.** Adjust the through cuts as needed to make sure they are uniform in size and shape. Draw the ornament design onto the back of the board. Be as accurate as you can so both sides are uniform.

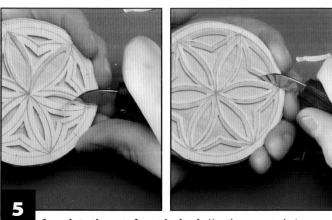

5 **Complete the cuts from the back.** Use the same techniques you used on the front to shave the pierced cuts out to the pattern lines. Carve or sand away any pattern lines on both sides of the ornament. Repeat the steps to make a matching ornament for the opposite side.

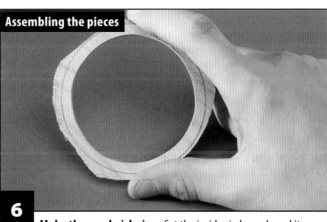

Assembling the pieces

6 **Make the sandwich ring.** Cut the inside circle, and sand it smooth. You can leave the sandwich ring solid for a sturdier ornament. Choose a different colored wood, such as butternut, or paint the ring for contrast. Apply the finish to the inside of the ring, and allow it to dry (see Finishing Notes).

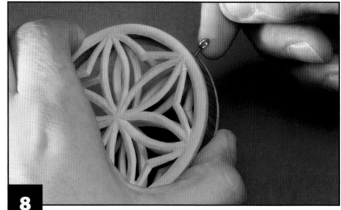

7 **Assemble the ornament.** Make a series of shallow divots on the inside rim of the chip carving with a sharp awl. This provides better glue adhesion. Apply wood glue to the rim, and center it on the sandwich ring. Clamp it in place and allow the glue to dry. Repeat the process to attach the opposite side.

8 **Sand the outside diameter of the ornament.** Remove any overhanging sandwich ring wood, and round the ornament on your sander of choice. I use a belt sander. Drill a pilot hole, and add a screw eye to the top for hanging the ornament. I use a small drop of glue to secure the screw eye in the ornament.

Finishing Notes

Aside from the inside of the sandwich ring, it is easiest to apply the finish after gluing the ornament together and sanding it to shape. Apply a light coat of Danish antiquing oil or your finish of choice to the ornament with a small artist's brush.

WORKING WITH WOOD GRAIN   **TIP**

Shift the centerline of the pattern about 15˚ clockwise or counterclockwise from the direction of the grain. It is difficult to cut with the grain without splitting the wood, so by shifting the pattern 15˚, most of your cuts will be diagonally across the grain.

Materials & Tools

Materials:

- 2 each ³⁄₃₂" x 3¼" x 3¼" basswood (pierced chip carvings)
- ¼" x 3¼" x 3¼" butternut or wood of choice (sandwich ring)
- ⅜" x 3¼" x 3¼" hardwood or plywood of choice (protective backing board)
- Drafting tools (mechanical pencil, eraser, small ruler, large plastic circle template) or carbon paper
- Danish antiquing oil or finish of choice

- Screw eyes
- Wood glue

Tools:

- Chip carving knife (I prefer a thin, hollow ground blade)
- Band saw, scroll saw, or saber saw
- Disc/belt sander or hand sander
- Small artist's brush
- Awl
- Clamps

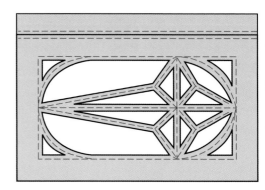

Angel Ornaments

By Barry McKenzie
Designed by Barry McKenzie

Most chip carving depends on the interaction of light and shadows in the bottom of the cuts; these beautiful ornaments take it to another level by introducing color to the chip carving.

It's an annual tradition for me to give away chip-carved angel Christmas ornaments to my friends and relatives. Since the angel told the shepherds that Jesus had been born, it's my little way of spreading the seasonal message.

After cutting out the perimeter of the ornaments from ¼"-thick stock, paint the face with several thick coats of non-metallic acrylic paint. I use vibrant colors such as red and blue. The natural color of the wood really stands out against these colors. After painting, slip a piece of graphite paper under the pattern and tape both pieces of paper in place with a bit of blue painter's tape. Then trace the chip carving pattern onto the blank.

Using standard chip carving techniques, carve through the paint to expose the natural wood. Be sure to brace your hand and make the curves smooth. The width of the chips should be even as well. Be sure your cuts meet at the bottom of the chip; otherwise you will not get a clean cut.

Photocopy at 135%

I pre-paint the front of some ornaments with acrylic craft paint and chip carve through the paint. While this does dull the blade faster (and requires me to sharpen more often), I like the contrast between the colored top and the light, unpainted wood in the chips. Remember, a traced-out free-form line pattern is only a guide, so let the knife blade track in the wood within or outside of the pattern lines. Because these are small enough to fit in your hand during carving, it's safer to have a backing piece of wood behind the ornament to protect the hand.

Materials & Tools

Materials:
- ¼" x 4" x 6" basswood blanks
- Non-metallic acrylic paints

- Paintbrush of choice

Tools:
- Chip carving knife of choice

SAFER CARVING   TIP

Cut two blanks the same size for each ornament, but only paint one. Use the other blank as a backing board while you hold and carve the other one. It prevents accidental cuts if the knife goes the whole way through the ornament.

Geometric Ornaments

By Roger Strautman

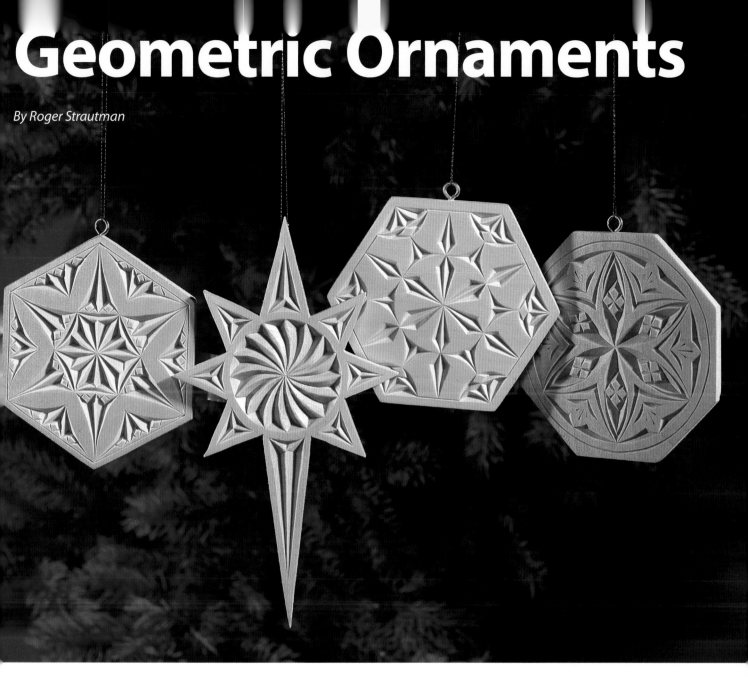

I find the overall shape of an ornament influences the interior chip design. In most cases, I find the center of an ornament and just start drawing. Experiment with different shapes and cuts to create your own designs.

You can draw the patterns directly on your blank with a .5mm pencil, a clear ruler, a compass, and a circle template. The patterns can also be traced on the blanks with graphite transfer paper.

I use a standard chip carving knife for most of the cuts. A stab knife is used to add decorative cuts on the flower-inspired ornaments. A device that provides light and magnification is helpful when working on small details.

After carving, apply your finish of choice. I use a gel stain and a satin lacquer finish. Allow the finish to dry and complete the ornament with a screw eye and hanging string.

Materials & Tools

Materials:
- ¼" x 3¼" x 3¾" basswood (A)
- ¼" x 3¾" x 6½" basswood (B)
- ¼" x 3½" x 3½" basswood (C)
- ¼" x 3¼" x 3¾" basswood (D)
- Small screw eyes (to hang ornament)
- Finish of choice (I use gel stain and satin lacquer)

Tools:
- Chip carving knife
- Stab knife (optional)
- Mechanical pencil, ruler, compass, circle template (to draw patterns)
- Graphite transfer paper or carbon paper (to trace patterns)
- Brushes to apply finish

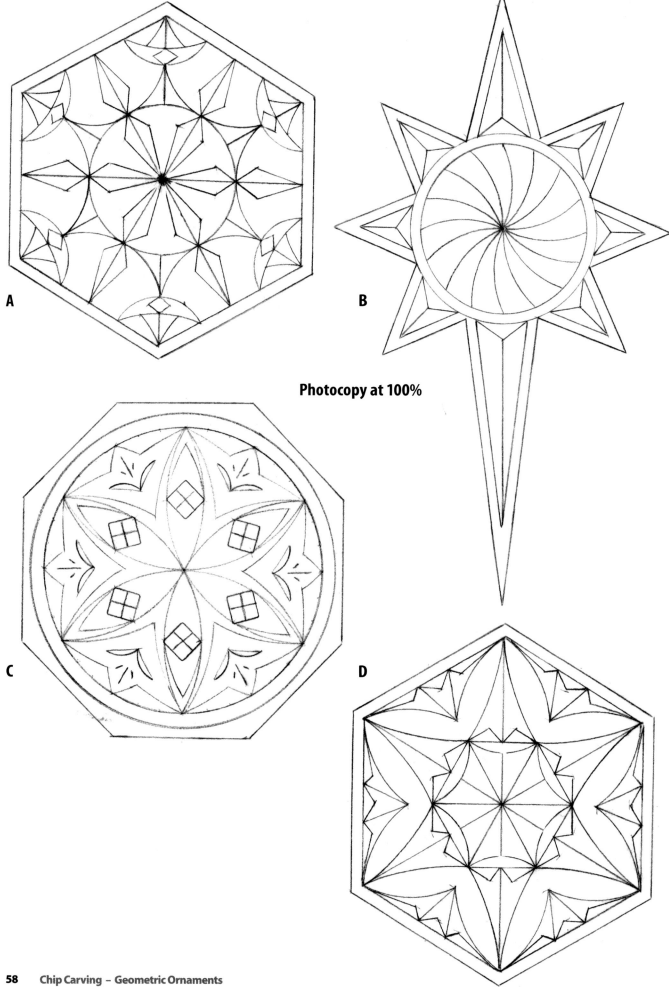

A

B

Photocopy at 100%

C

D

Holiday Patterns

By Roger Nancoz,
Photography by Roger Schroeder

All of my patterns are drawn using CorelDraw. The advantages of computer-generated designs are several. First, I can eliminate the need for mechanical aids when drawing a pattern. Second, it is very easy to create symmetrical or repetitive patterns. Third, the computer makes very fine lines—$^3/_{1000}$" wide. These features make for more precise chip carving. Although I create a variety of designs for plates, boxes, and special occasions, such as anniversaries, my holiday ornaments are especially popular.

Materials & Tools

Materials:

- ¼" x 4" diameter basswood (circular ornaments)
- ¼" x 3¾" x 3¾" basswood (dreidel)
- ¼" x 5½" x 5½" basswood (cross and star ornaments)
- Small screw eyes (to hang ornaments)
- Finish of choice

Tools:

- Chip carving knife
- Stab knife (optional)
- Mechanical pencil, ruler, compass, circle template (to draw patterns)
- Graphite transfer paper or carbon paper (to trace patterns)
- Brushes to apply finish

Hanukkah Menorah

I designed the Hanukkah menorah for my Jewish friends. The menorah is a good choice because of its clean lines. One of the two patterns has the shalom in Hebrew letters; the other uses the anglicized spelling.

Photocopy at 100%

The Dreidel

The dreidel, used during the Hanukkah festival, is a four-sided toy that spins like a top. Each side has a Hebrew letter. The pattern for my flat dreidel uses geometric designs and the four letters.

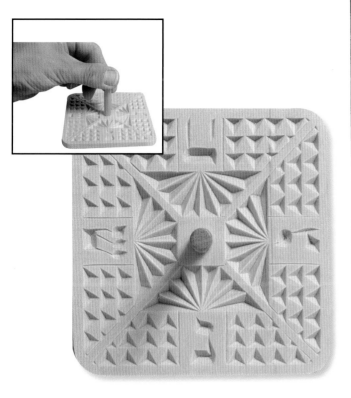

The Christmas Tree

The Christmas tree and the red color make this a holiday winner. Note that the branches of the tree are cut using two-sided chips.

Photocopy at 100%

Celtic Cross

My interpretation of the celtic cross is that the spirit of Christ radiates from the ends.

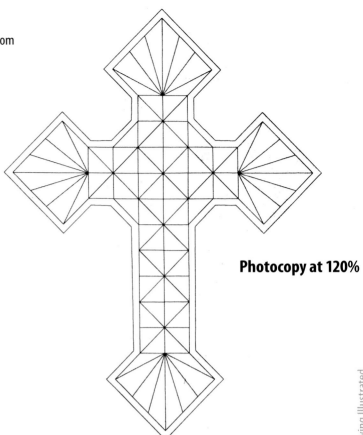

Photocopy at 120%

Star of Bethlehem

Four small stars surround the Star of Bethlehem. The blue color is popular with my customers. To prepare the wood for coloring, I sand it with 400-grit paper and then seal it with a spray lacquer. The last step is spraying the sealed surface with paint. I do wait at least four days for the paint to cure before I apply the pattern with rubber cement and cut through the cemented paper. After carving and shaping, the pattern is removed and the cement easily rubs off.

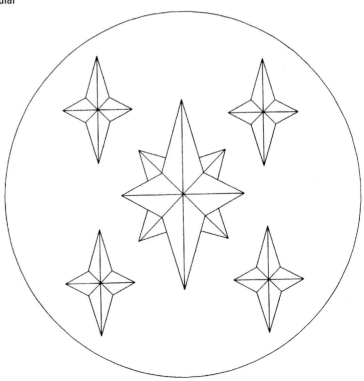

Photocopy at 100%

Eight–Point Star
The eight-point star has an unusual geometric pattern in its center. Although the chips are small, a sharp knife and fine lines make this one easier to carve than it appears.

Eight–Point Star
This eight-point star has a spiraling pattern—a classical design—in its center.

Photocopy at 100%

Projects

Whether you're looking for a decorative accent for your home, something for the outdoors, or a personalized gift to give away, you'll find it here. There is even a golf ball carving project to give you a chance to try a material other than wood. Use the information found in this section to create the projects and to give you finishing, carving, and other ideas for your future projects.

Floral Chip Carvings,
by Darrell Janssen, page 78.

Quilt Pattern Coasters

By Barry McKenzie

Learning to convert a variety of patterns into chip carving patterns will open up a whole new world of opportunities. Nearly any image can be converted into a free-form chip carving pattern, but quilt patterns are especially well-suited for geometric chip carved designs.

Books specializing in traditional quilt patterns are a rich source of inspiration. I found inspiration in a fabric quilt square created by my wife, Barbara. Once you are open to using patterns from other sources, you'll start to see chip carving patterns everywhere. Breaking these designs down into chip carving patterns is a good way to learn about pattern drafting and to study design concepts. This conversion process involves you more in the pattern. The pattern is no longer just random lines.

I've adapted a variety of quilt patterns to create this set of coasters. You can create an entire set using one design or mix and match the designs for a complete set. Each design uses a combination of standard chip carving techniques. Start by cutting your stock into 3½" squares and sanding out any surface irregularities. Then, trace or draw the pattern onto the blank.

One of the most helpful discoveries I have made in chip carving is how placing vertical stab cuts in the chip cavity provides control over the chip. Lateral displacement of the wood by the knife can cause breakout between chips. I control this lateral displacement by making vertical cuts inside the wood to be removed. With the stab cuts in place, the displacement created by the outlining cuts breaks the chips to pieces, producing perfectly shaped chips.

Pattern placement:

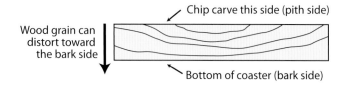

Wood grain can distort toward the bark side

Chip carve this side (pith side)

Bottom of coaster (bark side)

Wood tends to cup toward the bark side. Examine the end grain and carve on the pith side.

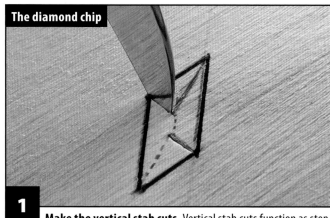

The diamond chip

1 **Make the vertical stab cuts.** Vertical stab cuts function as stop cuts. Cut at a 90° angle along the dotted lines. The dotted lines indicate the centerlines of the different segments of the chip. The line in the center denotes the deepest part of the chip.

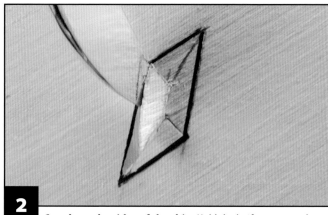

2 **Cut along the sides of the chip.** Hold the knife at any angle between 45° and 65°. The actual angle of entry is not critical as long as all of the angles of entry are identical. Cut down to the same depth on each of the cuts. The stab cuts break up the chip, making removal easy.

3 **Remove the chip.** Brush out the small broken pieces of the chip. Cut across the grain, with the knife held at the same angle, to remove any remaining wood inside the chip.

Geometric designs inspired by quilt patterns
make beautiful coasters.

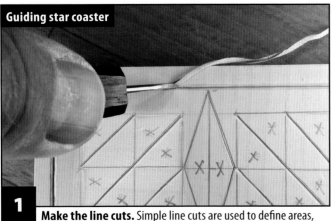

Guiding star coaster

1 Make the line cuts. Simple line cuts are used to define areas, such as the border, and to highlight the intersection of shallow chips. Angle your knife slightly and cut along both sides of the line. The cuts should intersect in the center at the deepest point of the chip. Free the chips at the corners.

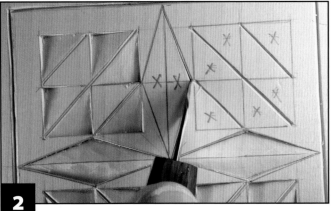

2 Make stop cuts on the two sides of the triangles. The stop cuts are deepest at the point of the triangle and taper to a very shallow cut at the base of the triangle. Most of these chips are less than ⅛" deep in the corner of the triangle.

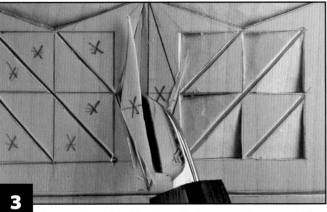

3 Remove the chips. Slice along the base up to the stop cuts. The depth of the cut is shallow at the base, but increases as you approach the point of the triangle. This slicing cut frees the chip. Depending on the depth of your chip, it may take two cuts to remove the entire chip.

Coaster caddy

Cut the pieces of the caddy to the sizes listed in the materials list. (Be sure to adjust the dimensions if you are adding felt to the coasters, as discussed below.) Cut 45° miters on the sides of the caddy where indicated on the pattern. Cut the finger cutouts on the sides with a band saw or scroll saw. Transfer the full pattern to the center of the long sides. Fold the full pattern along the dotted line and transfer the pattern to the blanks, aligning the fold with the mitered ends of all four side pieces. Chip carve the designs before assembly. Apply wood glue to the sides of the base and to the miters on the side pieces. Place all six pieces in position and clamp them in place until the glue dries.

Finishing notes

Because wet glasses will be placed on the coasters, they need to be protected. Pay attention to the end grain of the wood when finishing, as it is more porous and will absorb more finish.

For the first coat of finish, dilute one part tabletop varnish with an equal amount of mineral spirits. The thinned varnish will penetrate deeper into the wood. Allow the finish to dry overnight. If the finish bubbles, sand with used 400-grit or finer sandpaper. Keep the finish mixture in a jar and use a stencil-size brush that can be stored inside the closed jar; that way you will not need to clean your brush each time. Add a bit of extra varnish to the mixture and apply a second coat of finish.

After the second coat has dried, apply a light stain to the chip cavities. Wipe off the stain immediately. Allow the stain to dry overnight. Add more varnish to the finish mixture and apply a third coat. Brush the finish onto the wood with the grain and do not let the finish puddle up in the chip cavities. Tilt the coaster this way and that in a well-lit area to make sure the finish is consistent and bubble-free. After the finish dries, apply a light coat of the thinned varnish to the back of the coasters. You can leave the coasters as they are or attach small self-adhesive felt dots. Remember, you will need to adjust the dimensions of the coaster caddy if you add the felt. Polish the varnish with a crumpled-up brown paper bag or used dryer sheets.

Clean your hands and the brushes with dishwashing liquid. The coaster caddy can be sealed using your finish of choice. I use a tung oil finish.

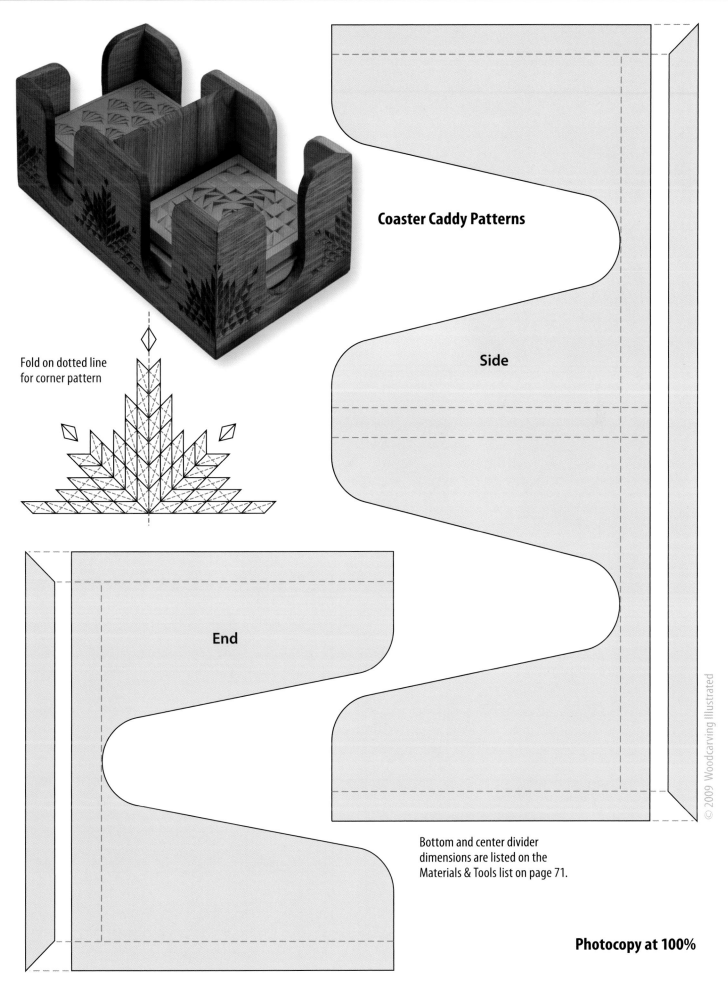

Coaster Caddy Patterns

Side

End

Fold on dotted line for corner pattern

Bottom and center divider dimensions are listed on the Materials & Tools list on page 71.

Photocopy at 100%

Coaster Patterns

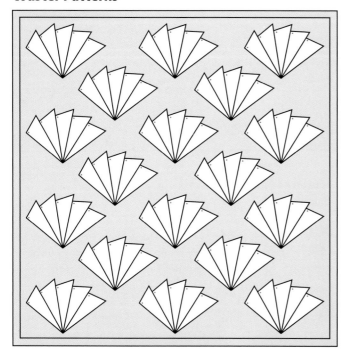

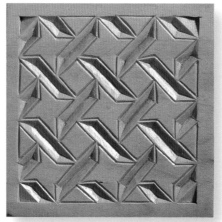

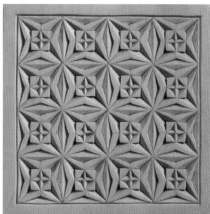

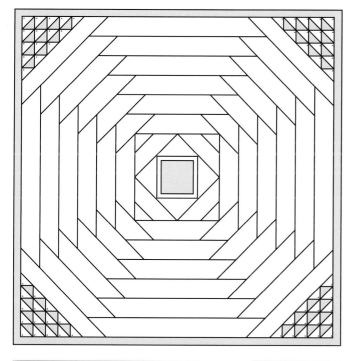

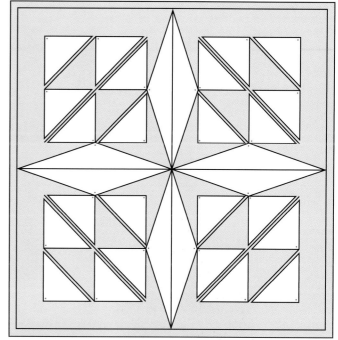

Photocopy at 100%

Materials:

- 12 each ⅜" x 3½" x 3½" basswood or wood of choice (coasters)
- 2 each ⅜" x 3⁷⁄₁₆" x 4⅜" butternut or wood of choice (short coaster caddy ends)
- 2 each ⅜" x 3⁷⁄₁₆" x 8⁵⁄₁₆" butternut or wood of choice (long coaster caddy sides)

- ⅜" x 2⅞" x 3¾" butternut or wood of choice (coaster caddy center divider)
- ⅜" x 3¾" x 7⅝" butternut or wood of choice (coaster caddy bottom)
- Tabletop varnish, high gloss
- Tung oil satin finish

- Golden oak stain or light stain of choice
- Used 400-grit or finer sandpaper (remove bubbles in finish)
- Crumpled-up brown paper bag or used dryer sheets (polish finish)
- Self-adhesive felt dots (optional)

Materials & Tools

Tools:

- Chip carving knife of choice
- Ruler, square, and mechanical pencil (to draw pattern) or graphite paper (to trace pattern)
- Stencil-size brush (to apply finish)
- Rags (to wipe up excess finish)

Chip Carving on Eggs

By Diane Harto,
Photography by Bob Wilson

Chip carving must begin with an extremely sharp knife. Without a properly sharpened one, I get nowhere. My favorite type of knife has a small, narrow blade with a tapered, flexible tip.

As with any chip-carved project, I start by sanding the surface thoroughly, sometimes with a sanding drum first, then by hand with 220-grit sandpaper. Next, I draw the pattern directly onto the egg. Transferring a flat pattern onto a round surface just won't work.

My pattern begins with a vertical line from the top of the egg to the bottom. To space the lines evenly, I use a thin strip of paper as if it were a flexible ruler. I mark the top and the bottom of the line on the paper, then fold the paper to find the center. I use the same procedure to mark the horizontal lines. I continue doing this until I have a grid over the entire surface of the egg.

I take a minute or two to decide if I want to go with a totally geometric design or a more free-form one. There is lots of room to be creative here. I can divide the squares of my grid with diagonal lines, curved lines, or both. I can repeat the pattern all around or do something different in each square. However, I tend to keep the shapes on the small side because carving on a rounded surface can be tricky. Making long cuts around the egg, for example, is difficult. Once I had done several eggs, I had a better idea of what small really meant.

I like to leave what I call "air space" in my designs. An occasional break in the pattern gives me a place to change direction when the round shape hinders my carving. It also makes for a more appealing design when the egg is finished.

Carving starts at the top or narrow end of the egg. As I move through the cuts, I make sure to follow the round surface as well as the pattern lines. This is very different from carving on a flat surface. An obstacle I encounter, however, is the end grain at the top. The wood in this area tends to crumble easily if my knife is the slightest bit dull or if the egg has not been sanded smooth.

I move across and around the egg, following the pattern in an organized manner. Chip carving an egg is not a haphazard operation. I compare it to playing chess, where I think about the next cut so I don't corner myself into a place from which there is nowhere to go.

I also carve toward the widest circumference of the egg and stop. With some of my designs, I have a break at this point. I find it best to carve toward the widest area because if I carve toward the narrow ends, a lot of breaking and splintering occurs. I want to carve into the thickness of the wood rather than the thinner, recessed shape of the ends. I continue carving until the entire egg is finished.

Finishing Up

When the carving is completed, I like to finish the egg with tung oil. After painting on the oil with a brush to get it into the deep cuts, I wipe the flat surfaces with a cloth. Once the egg has had a chance to dry overnight, I use 0000 (4/0) steel wool to rub down the wood. Since the chips tend to fill up with fragments of the steel wool, I brush them out with an old toothbrush. I repeat this process until I have four or five coats of tung oil on the egg. After the last coat of oil, I do not rub with steel wool at all. I just allow the wood to dry.

Another finishing method I use is to wipe on tung oil with a cloth only on the flat surfaces, deliberately not going into the deep chips. I do this twice, allowing each application to dry overnight. Once dry, I brush the egg with a thin wash of stain or acrylic paint, making sure to get it into the chips. I wipe the stain off the flat surfaces, allow the egg to dry, and repeat the process until I have the finish I find most appealing.

Some carvers recommend applying the finish first, then chip carve. I believe this can have a dulling effect on the knife as I carve through a hardened finish.

LAST CUT FIRST   **TIP**

When I carve an area that has chips on all sides—a rosette, for example—it is helpful to make what will be my last cut ahead of time. I am less likely to break out the wall of that chip when I finally cut near it. I call this method last cut first.

Making a grid

1 **Make the vertical lines.** When laying out the pattern for a chip carved egg, I start by using a strip of paper as if it were a ruler. By marking on the paper the top and bottom of the egg, I find the center of the egg simply by folding the paper in half.

2 **Make the horizontal lines.** I use the same procedure when laying out the horizontal lines. Here I connect the center points on the vertical lines.

3 **Draw your pattern.** My patterns range from the geometric to the free form, and sometimes a combination of both.

4 **Double-check that the shapes are small.** I keep the shapes small because of the difficulty of making long cuts on a round surface.

5 **Leave "air spaces."** Pictured are two stages of how I develop my patterns. I try to leave what I call air spaces—the horizontal stripes—in the patterns. Being able to change carving direction at one of these spaces is helpful when working on a round surface. The air spaces also make for a more appealing design.

Carving

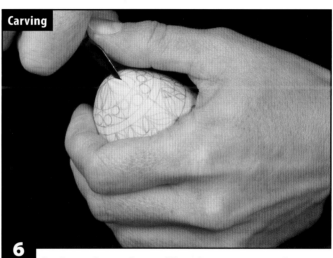

6 **Begin carving at the top.** When chip carving an egg, I start at the top or narrow end and follow the grain as much as I can.

7 **Work toward the middle.** I carve from the top down to the widest circumference, then change direction and work from the bottom of the egg toward the middle.

CARVE AWAY PENCIL LINES **TIP**

One of the goals I have for my chip carvings is to carve away all the pencil marks. If I accomplish this, it is a good bet that my chip walls will come to sharp peaks rather than flat spaces between cuts. It also means little or no erasing, which can cause chip walls to break. I use this as a gauge for how my skills have improved. The fewer the pencil marks left, the better my chip carving.

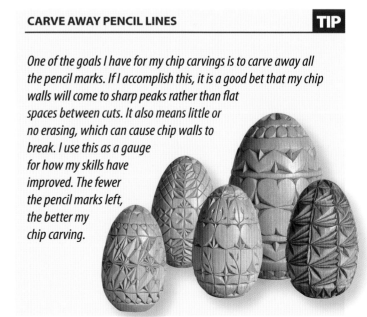

Landscape

By Barry McKenzie

In the past, wood that had blemishes, discolorations, stress lines, or remnants of knotholes would have been discarded or burned. But a closer look at this wood reveals images in the wood grain that can be interpreted as a landscape or sea scene.

Using some imagination while looking at this wood grain is like looking at cloud formations and seeing all sorts of images and scenes in the clouds.

Each board reveals something different with no two pieces being the same. The Dutch have used these pieces of wood for years, embellishing them with just a few chip cuts to enhance the scene. When creating landscape art, I follow these basic rules:

- Find wood that has unique characteristics. With a few embellishments, it can become a work of art.
- The location of the tree will represent the land mass.
- Look for a place on the wood where the tree roots will have something to lock onto, such as a knothole or dark spot on the surface of the wood.
- Add a few birds (three preferably) grouped together. Make them different sizes representing the near and far, to give the landscape depth and to identify the sky above the horizon.
- Let your child-like imagination run free, and let the wood grain speak for itself.

Finding tree shapes

There are a variety of places where you can find tree shapes suitable for this style of landscape chip carving. You want a single standing tree that has been affected by nature and the weather. It should not be symmetrical, and should have a very individual form. You can find trees like this on top of mountains, on sea coasts, or on the rim of large canyons. You can also look up photos of bonsai trees on the internet or in a library. Finish the landscape with a frame made of old wood.

FREE FORM = FREEDOM TIP

Being a free-form style chip project, there is no set pattern you have to follow. Anything that you carve will look good!

The Cuts

This unique chip is usually found in Egyptian-type sandstone carving that produces a relief image in the surface of the carving. It has the look of a Japanese landscape painting—a mystical, old, weathered look.

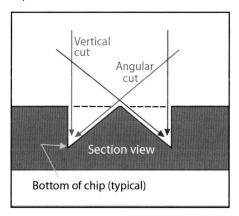

Start with a vertical cut along both sides of the outside of a portion of the tree. Then make an angular cut from the center of the width, converging the angular cut with the vertical cut.

Step 1: Transfer the pattern to the workpiece. Size the pattern to fit your blank. Tape a piece of graphite paper face down on the wood. Then tape the pattern on top of the graphite paper. Trace over the pattern with a red pen or slip a piece of wax paper over the pattern so you know where you have already traced without having to lift the pattern and transfer paper.

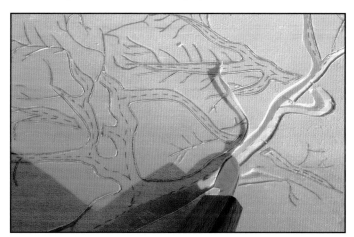

Step 2: Make the vertical cut. Make vertical cuts along the entire profile of the tree. Do not outline the limbs if they get too narrow or too close; these areas will be removed with angular cuts from both sides. Go back over the vertical cuts a few times to give the cuts some depth.

Step 3: Make the angular cuts. Start in the center of the width, and cut down at an angle to the bottom of the vertical cuts made in Step 2. Sometimes it is better to start the cut with a shallow cut near the vertical cut. Then go back and make the cut deeper and wider until you reach the center of the tree or branch width. Detail the smaller branches with two angular cuts. Finish the branches with a few stab cuts to simulate thin twigs and leaves.

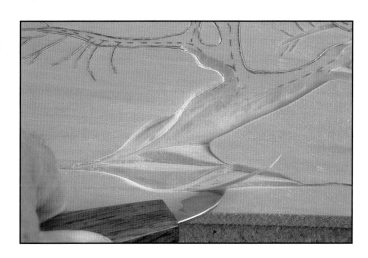

Step 4: Detail the trunk and roots of the tree. On the main project, I locate the tree over a knot, which anchors the tree to the land mass. If you don't have a knot or discoloration to anchor the tree, make a few vertical and angular cuts perpendicular to the trunk to anchor the tree to the land profile.

Finishing

I lightly stain parts of my landscape scenes to highlight certain surfaces or to separate the land from the sky. After carving, apply a few coats of your finish of choice to seal the wood. This will keep the stain from soaking into the wood too deeply. Apply the stain, and immediately wipe it off the areas you don't want it with a damp rag. A small paint brush can also be used to feather the stain out to lessen the contrast between the stained and unstained wood. It is all a matter of personal preference.

Materials & Tools

Materials:
- Landscape board of choice
- Graphite transfer paper
- Wax paper (optional)
- Red pen (optional)
- Tape
- Finish of choice
- Stain of choice
- Old-wood picture frame (optional)
- Small paint brush

Tools:
- Chip carving knife of choice

SPECIAL SOURCES:

Barry McKenzie has put together a landscape chip carving kit complete with a landscape board and booklet of tree silhouette shapes.

Contact him at 23427 Route 66, Lebanon, MO 65536-5325,

417-532-8438,

www.chipcarvingschool.com.

Floral Chip Carvings

By Darrell Janssen

Sometimes less is more when it comes to chip carving—these classy designs can be made with one knife and just a few cuts. They've been popular at every show I've displayed them.

If you are carving a plaque, cut your blank to the desired size. Then, sand it with progressively finer grits of sandpaper up to 400 grit. Transfer the pattern to the blank by putting graphite or carbon paper under the pattern and tracing it onto the blank.

These original floral designs are a great way to add a decorative touch to almost any project.

CHIP CARVED CABINETS

These floral chip carvings are a great design element to add to your home. I've carved floral designs into a number of plaques sized to fit on the doors of my kitchen cabinets.

I chose to add plaques onto the doors because you want a wood with a clear and consistant grain when you are chip carving; otherwise it's difficult to get clean cuts. Since I didn't know what I would find once I started carving the cabinet doors, I carved plaques from select lumber.

Another reason I added the plaques instead of carving the doors is because it's easier to replace a plaque if you make a miscut than it is to replace a cabinet door.

The chip carved plaques were cut to the same proportion for each door, since many of the doors were of assorted sizes.

Carving the Designs

Step 1: Divide the larger leaves in half. Use the center vein or rib of the leaf as a guide for this centerline. When making the radius cuts on the large end, cut inside your lines first. You want to get a feel for keeping the cut of the knife smooth while you complete the turn. When you have a feel for the technique, go back, enlarge the cuts to the lines, and remove any imperfections from your practice cuts. Hold your knife at a lower angle—this helps you make a smoother cut. Use this same technique to carve the grass-shaped leaves. Make all of the cuts except for the blossoms.

Step 2: Make one continuous circular cut for the center of the blossom. Carve the petals in a similar manner as the leaves; again, cut inside the lines to get the feel for the curves. In order for the blossoms to look realistic, the cuts need to be clean, regularly repeated, and symmetrical. Make practice cuts on all the blossoms. Go back, and cut out to the line to clean up any imperfections.

Step 3: Sand the edges of the blank. Use 400-grit sandpaper to round over the corners.

Step 4: Clean off any dust. Use compressed air or a tack cloth.

Step 5: Finish as desired. Use a stain, oil finish, or lacquer of choice.

Making a Custom Basket Lid

A basket with a custom carved lid makes a thoughtful gift. Once you've created the blank for the lid, the chip carved design is a quick way to make the project unique.

Step 1: Choose your basket. I use baskets that have a rigid, banded top edge. This edge serves as a platform to keep the lid flat and gives you a snug fit around the lid.

Step 2: Make a pattern for the basket. Turn the basked upside down on a piece of poster paper, and trace around the edge. Cut out the poster board, and trace around it onto a ¾"-thick blank (I use basswood). Then, measure the thickness of the basket rim—if it is thicker than ⅜"-thick, reduce the size of the lid until a ⅜"-deep rabbet around the inside of the lid will fit inside the basket.

Size to fit blank of choice

Rue-Anemone

Step 3: Cut out the basket lid. For square lids, a table saw works best, but for round lids, you will need to use a band saw, scroll saw, or jigsaw. Sand the piece to shape.

Step 4: Add the rabbet. Use a router to add a ⅜"-deep rabbet around the entire perimeter of the lid. Test the fit and sand any places where it doesn't fit. Remember, you want the lid to fit snugly.

Step 5: Sand the lid with progressively finer grits of sandpaper up to 400-grit. Then, carve it using the same techniques you used for the plaque.

Materials & Tools

Materials:
- ¾" basswood or wood of choice at size of choice
- Sandpaper, various grits up to 400 grit
- Finish of choice (I suggest stain, oil finish or laquer)
- Poster board (for basket pattern)

Tools:
- Chip carving knife of choice

- Ruler and mechanical pencil (to draw pattern)
- Saw of choice (to cut wood to size)
- Tack rag or compressed air
- Brushes or rags (for applying finish)

© 2009 Woodcarving Illustrated

**Size to fit blank
of choice**

Star-of-Bethlehem

INSPIRED BY NATURE

I was looking for other ideas to carve on basket lids after I had done a bundle of wheat on a lid for a basket shaped for a loaf of French bread. From my bookshelf, I started looking through a copy of the Peterson Field Guide of Wildflowers. I started sketching simple line drawings of violets, wood sorrel, and trumpet vine. Not all wildflowers can be chip carved because of the delicate design in their leaves or blossoms. I have found that simpler is better to start with.

During a visit to Jamestown, N.Y., recently, I made a point to see the Roger Tory Peterson Institute. While there I talked with staff members about my using the Peterson book as a resource. I was welcomed to use these pictures to sketch from as long as I did no copying.

Chess Set

By Barry McKenzie

Chess was invented in India around the sixth century A.D. This set combines one of the oldest forms of carving with one of the oldest board games. Although the set is highly decorative and makes a beautiful display, it is fully functional and quite durable.

I use standard design elements to distinguish the pieces. The king has a cross on top, connecting it with the Crusades. The queen has a crown identifying her royalty. The knight is a stylized representation of a knight's horse. The bishop has a top much like a pope's miter. The rook's top represents the ramparts of a medieval castle wall.

The completed set looks impressive, but in reality, you only need to master five basic cuts. The trick is reproducing these cuts consistently. I used simple chips to embellish the game board, but it could be left as a solid surface. The design for the board squares is rotated and repeated to create the overall pattern.

I used basswood and butternut for my set. Both woods are well suited for chip carving. You could carve the entire set from basswood and use stains to distinguish the opposing sides.

Five Basic Chip Cuts

Start by cutting the chess piece blanks. For most pieces, that entails sawing them to size and tapering them using a disc sander or a belt sander. Sand the blanks with progressively finer grits of sandpaper up to 220-grit. Transfer the patterns to the blanks. I like to draw the designs onto the blanks using a ruler and a mechanical pencil, but you can also use graphite transfer paper and a stylus.

Five basic chip cuts will complete the chess set. Practice the cuts on scrap wood until you are comfortable that you can reproduce them consistently. Don't feel you have to complete the entire set at once. Carve a few pieces then take a break with a different project.

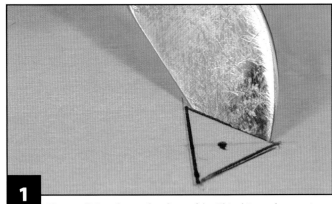

1 **The traditional angular deep chip.** This chip can be any size, as long as the cuts all converge at the deepest point in the middle of the chip. Hold the knife at the same angle to make all of the cuts. After you free the chip, go back and lightly carve into the corner to remove any splintered wood and clean up the chip.

2 **The shallow chip.** Draw the chip the same as the angular deep chip, but cut it differently. Make vertical cuts on both sides of the triangle. The deepest cuts are at the triangle's point and decrease in depth as you approach the triangle's base. Hold the knife nearly horizontal and cut from one side of the base to the other, while sliding the tip of the knife up to the deepest part of the chip at the tip of the triangle.

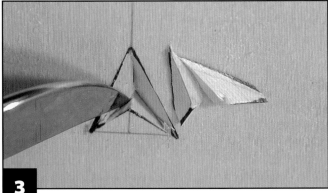

3 **Old-world-style chip.** Traditionally made using chisels, gouges, and skew knives, this chip can be made with a chip carving knife. It requires two angular cuts and two vertical cuts. Hold the knife at an angle and cut along the two sides of the large triangle toward the point of the small triangle. Make two vertical cuts along the sides of the small triangle to release the chip. Do not remove the wood for the small triangle.

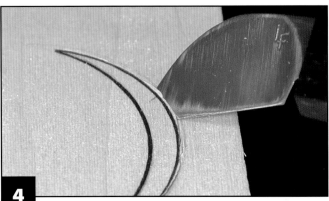

4 **Flare or free-form angular line cut.** Establish the bottom of the chip with the first cut, and free the chip with the second cut. The angle at which you hold the blade changes depending on the depth and width of the line. As the chip gets deeper, the angle increases until the knife is nearly vertical. For the shallow areas, the angle decreases until the knife is nearly horizontal.

5 **Straight line cut.** Establish the bottom of the chip with the first cut and release the chip with the second cut. Depending on the width of the line, you may need to make short cuts on either end of the line to free the chip. The blade is held at an identical angle when making all of the cuts. The depth of the cut is the same from end to end.

Finishing

My main objective is to seal the wood around the top surface of the chip cavity before more finish is added to the chip. This will keep the chips looking crisp and clean-cut. If finish gets down in the chips without sealing around the chip cavity first, the finish will bleed or weep out from the edges of the chip cavity, giving the chip a dull, muted look.

Step 1: Seal the main surface. Brush a light amount of finish on the exterior surface, avoiding the chip cavities. Use a ½"-wide, stiff artists' brush. Tilt the wood to reflect light off the surface and spot any areas missing finish or stain. Let it dry.

Step 2: Seal the edges of the chips. Brush additional finish on the surface, getting some finish around the top edge of the chip cavities, but not inside the cavities. Swipe a damp brush across the top of the chips. Let the finish dry.

Step 3: Add finish to the chip cavities. Wet the surface much more than the first two applications, and get some finish down inside the top edge of the cavities. Do not flood the cavity. Swipe a wet brush across the top and slightly over the edge of the cavity. Let the finish dry.

Step 4: Flood the chip cavity. Fill the cavities with finish. Before the finish starts to dry, wipe off the surface, the top of the chips, and down in the cavities with a soft rag. Continue brushing with a dry brush to remove the excess finish. Let it dry.

Step 5: Accent the chip cavities. Flood the chip cavities with light-colored stain, and immediately remove as much finish as possible with a rag. Then, brush with a dry brush until you remove all of the finish from the cavities. Let it dry. This step is optional.

Step 6: Apply a second coat of finish. If the chip cavities look dull, flood the cavities with more finish. Remove as much finish as possible with a rag, and brush the chips with a dry brush to remove all of the finish from the cavities. You can apply an additional coat to give the project a high-gloss finish.

THE GAME BOARD

Cut nine 1" x 1¾" x 15¾" strips, five of basswood and four of butternut. Glue them together in an alternating pattern. After the glue has dried, cut the blank into eight 1¾"-wide strips (the extra length offsets the wood removed by the saw with each cut). Offset the strips by one entire square to produce the alternating dark and light pattern. Glue the strips in place, then cut off the overhanging squares.

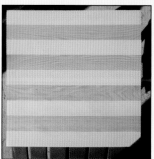

CARVING THE GAME BOARD

All of the squares use the same pattern, but the image used to embellish the dark squares is rotated 90° to create an overall pattern for the entire board. Use a shallow chip technique to remove the light areas of the pattern. You can also embellish the chips with a thin, shallow line cut at the base of the triangles.

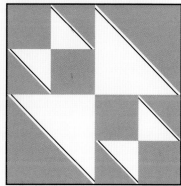

This pattern is used for both white and dark squares.

To complete the game board and give it a polished look, miter-cut commercial molding and edge glue them around the squares to serve as a frame.

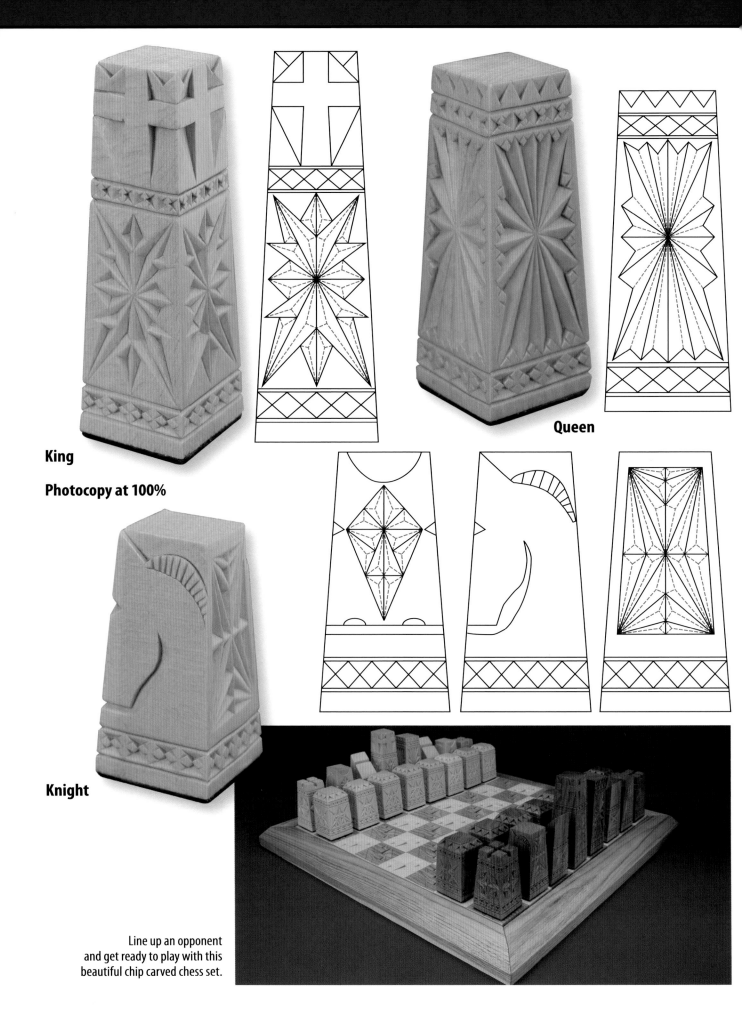

King

Photocopy at 100%

Queen

Knight

Line up an opponent
and get ready to play with this
beautiful chip carved chess set.

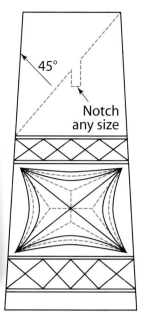

45°

Notch
any size

Bishop

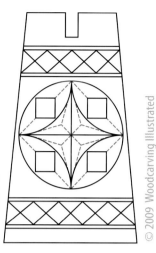

Rook

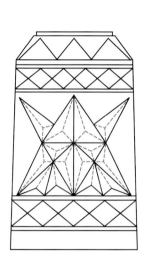

Photocopy at 100%

Pawn

Materials&Tools

Materials:
- 1⅜" x 1⅜" x 43" basswood (light pieces)
- 1⅜" x 1⅜" x 43" butternut (dark pieces)
- 5 each 1" x 1¾" x 15¾" basswood (light squares)
- 4 each 1" x 1¾" x 15¾" butternut (dark squares)
- Assorted grits of sandpaper up to 220 grit
- Low gloss or clear satin oil finish of choice
- Polyurethane finish of choice

- Light-colored gel stain of choice (optional)
- Finishing rags

Tools:
- Chip carving knife of choice
- Saw of choice (to cut pieces and board squares)
- Disc sander or belt sander
- Paintbrushes of choice

Chip Carved Golf Balls

By Sharon Braunberger

Carving golf balls is addictive! They are easier to carve than wood, and a lot more forgiving, but they dull your knife faster. Removing the cover is the most difficult part. You never know what color you will find inside.

You can display the chip carved golf balls on their own as a striking Christmas ornament, but I prefer to showcase mine in a matching cage with a clock or photo insert. The completed project is a real conversation starter.

For this clock, I carve the same heart design on the three sides that don't have the clock insert on them. You can also carve a different design on each side. I maintained the same heart design for the golf ball. You can use the basic techniques to craft a variety of different clocks.

Many manufacturers who sell clock inserts also sell miniature photo frames.

To begin, transfer your pattern to the blank. Some chip carvers trace the pattern onto the blank, but I prefer to draw it on with a ruler; it just gives me a cleaner carving. When laying out the pattern, you can make a variation of my design by switching the heart border on the bottom with the large heart/clock insert on the top.

Preparing the blank

1

Drill holes to open up the cage. I use a 15/16"-diameter Forstner bit to drill the whole way through the block. Drill two holes per side to clear as much of the waste out as possible. Since this is the same size drill bit that you need for the clock/photo insert, drill those holes as well, but don't drill the whole way through the block.

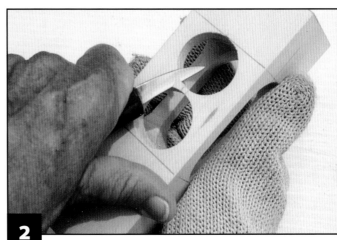

2

Carve away the excess wood between the holes. You want the oval on each side to be the same size. Sand the inside of the cage with 220-grit sandpaper. At this point, you can move on to the golf ball. Remove the cover, using your method of choice (See page 89 for golf ball carving tips).

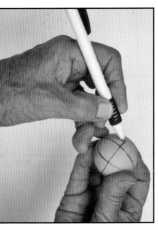

3 **Divide the golf ball.** Divide the ball into four equal sections. Then, divide these sections in half, so you have eight sections. Draw a center line across these eight divisions. Draw six circles with an equal diameter on the ball (four across the diameter and one on the top and bottom).

4 **Draw on the hearts.** Use the lines you've already drawn on the ball as a guide. Then divide each quarter of the heart into sections. The quarters in the bottom section are divided into three sections and the quarters on the top half are divided into four sections.

5 **Draw a standard chip carving pattern into the top and bottom circle.** Carve the design using standard chip carving techniques. Make a deep triangular chip cut between the hearts at the bottom of the ball. Cut three shallow triangles inside each of these deep triangles. Carve away the triangles between the top of the heart and the top pattern.

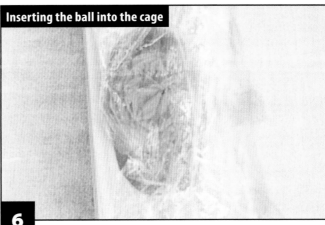

Inserting the ball into the cage

6 **Insert the golf ball into the cage.** Soak the cage in water for about 10 minutes. Add the screw hook to the top of the ball and wrap the ball in a plastic bag or plastic wrap. Press the ball into the cage with an even pressure. Sometimes the cage still cracks, which is why I wait to chip carve the cage. Remove the plastic wrap, and let the cage dry for 6 to 8 hours.

7 **Lay out the pattern on the cage.** I use a ¼" grid. Make marks ¼" apart down the length of each corner. Transfer the heart patterns to the top and bottom of each side, except where the clock insert/photo frame will be located. Use the pattern as a reference. Carve the heart designs first. Then, make the angular cuts on the corners.

8 **Add a screw eye to the top of the cage (on the inside).** Use a very short length of chain to link the ball with the cage. You want the ball to hang in the center of the cage. Apply your finish of choice. I apply a brush-on varnish, because it gets deeper into the cuts. After the finish dries, install the clock or photo inserts.

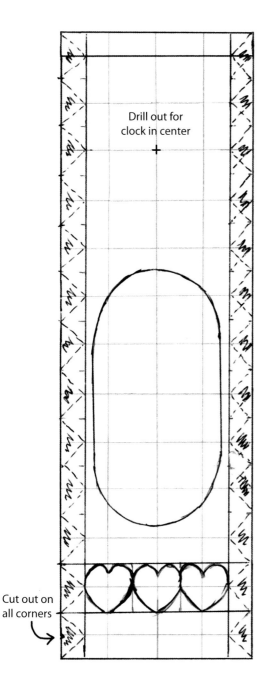

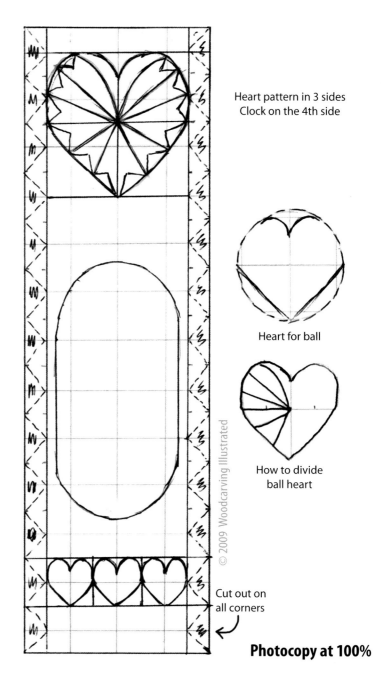

Drill out for
clock in center

Heart pattern in 3 sides
Clock on the 4th side

Heart for ball

How to divide
ball heart

Cut out on
all corners

Cut out on
all corners

© 2009 Woodcarving Illustrated

Photocopy at 100%

X MARKS THE SPOT   **TIP**

*Mark your first cut with an X because it will close up after
you make the cut. Clean off the pen marks by sanding the
ball lightly or soaking it in a diluted bleach solution.*

Materials&**Tools**

Materials:
- 2" x 2" x 6½" basswood
- Golf ball of choice
- 2 small screw eyes
- 1" length of small chain
- Clock or picture insert
- Brush on varnish
- Sandpaper, assorted grits

Tools:
- Chip carving knife
  or detail knife of choice
- Pen
- Pencil
- Compass
- Ruler

Tips for making the most of this interesting medium

By Elaine Dugan

The hardest part about carving a golf ball is getting the cover off. Golf ball cores are easier to carve than wood.

You can carve any number of things in the center of the solid-core golf balls, and they come in so many bright colors. Caricature carvers have been carving faces in them for quite some time, so I decided to try chip carving one.

I've come up with a few techniques to make carving golf balls even easier.

GOLF BALL MARKING JIG

Whether you are making an intricate chip carving design or a caricature face, it is important to divide the golf ball into sections. This will help you maintain proper proportions. I've devised a simple jig to help you mark your carving.

Transfer the jig pattern to a 1½"-thick piece of scrap wood. Drill a 1½"-diameter hole ¾"-deep where indicated on the pattern. A golf ball should sit inside the hole half way, so it is easy to divide the core into two hemispheres. Then mark the divisions onto the golf ball. Rotate the ball until the marks line up with the surface of the wood. Then draw the division line from end to end of the golf ball. This is much easier than trying to hold a ruler against the golf ball.

Side view

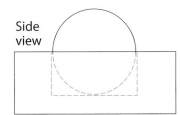

Top view

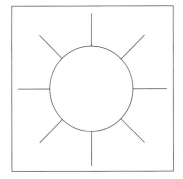

Removing the Cover

Step 1: Cut through the cover. Mark around the center of the golf ball with a permanent marker. Use a sharp carving knife or a rotary power carver equipped with a cutting wheel. Cut around the center line, but try to keep from cutting too deeply into the core of the golf ball. Hold the golf ball tightly in a carving glove, or wrap a towel or hot pad around it to protect your hands. Then, make a series of cuts in the opposite direction. Divide each hemisphere into three sections, like slicing a pie.

Step 2: Slide a flat screwdriver under the cover, and pry the cover off. Once you loosen up a corner, grab the cover with a pair of pliers. If it's difficult to remove, drop it in a cup of boiling water for a minute or two.

Step 3: Appraise the core. I only carve golf balls that are a pretty color. Some are a bland brown or green; I discard those. I like the bright pink, purple, orange, green, and blue ones.

Marking Your Chip Carving Design

Step 1: Mark the seam with a ballpoint pen. Most golf balls have a recognizable seam that splits the core into two hemispheres. Do not use a pencil, because it rubs off too easily. Likewise, do not use a gel-type pen, which soaks into the core. Divide the two hemispheres into equal parts by drawing three lines parallel to the center line about ¼" apart.

Step 2: Divide the golf ball into sections from the other direction. You will be dividing the golf ball into 8 pie-shaped sections. You can use a ruler, but many people have made a simple jig to hold and mark the golf ball. Once your grid is in place, you can use it to draw in your chip carving design.

Finishing Your Golf Ball Carving

Step 1: Clean the carving. Start with an all-purpose cleaner, such as Formula 409 or Fantastic. If any pen marks remain, drop the golf ball into a diluted solution of water and bleach. Allow it to dry thoroughly.

Step 2: Add the tiny screw eye. Make a tiny V-shaped cut in the top of the golf ball core with your carving knife to get the screw eye started. Thread a matching ribbon through the screw eye, and knot it as a hanger.

Wedding Plate

By Barry McKenzie

A handcrafted, chip carved wedding plate is one of those special gifts a couple receives that shows someone cared enough to spend their time creating a personalized gift made especially for them. It will certainly have more meaning than the store-bought appliances that are traditionally given as wedding gifts. The plate works equally as well as an anniversary gift.

The chip used is a unique shallow chip you learn to do as you go along. It's unlike what you might be experienced in doing, but don't give up on it. This chip doesn't come out in one piece, but with a series of shallow shave cuts.

Start by transferring the pattern to the blank. The chip carving pattern is simply traced on. The lettering, since you are personalizing it, takes a little bit of thought (see Chip Carved Letters).

1 **Make stop cuts from the deep end of the chip.** These cuts stop the shaving cuts. Cut them as deep as you can. Keep the vertical cuts angling out from the point of the chip. Insert the tip of the blade into the corner, and drag the cut to the other end. Continue making shallow, horizontal slices until you reach the midpoint of the diamond-shaped chip.

2 **Refine and deepen the chip.** Start by cutting deeper stop cuts. These second stop cuts are needed to allow you to keep shaving the chip deeper. Continue shaving and deepening the chips. This is where the convex-shaped blade is more useful. (See Use the Right Knife for the Job). Continue this process on all chips, working from the center of the circle out toward the perimeter.

Joyce & Roger

December 30, 2005

This unique, shallow-chip design
is accented by the classic leaf design
featured on page 40.

Chip Carved Letters

I suggest beginners use a Unical-based lettering for their plate. Old English lettering is difficult to read, and script lettering is hard to chip carve. I've included my modification of the American Unical font adapted for chip carving.

On my plate, I used Matura MJ Script Lettering, but I was confident that I would be able to carve it. The Unical lettering looks equally nice.

The easiest way to transfer the letters to the workpiece is to decide where to locate the bottom of the letters on the radius of the plate. Then, lightly trace the letters, one at a time, onto the rim of the plate, using graphite paper. Do not use carbon paper. Carbon paper is wax based and will be impossible to erase. Graphite paper can be erased easily.

The words should be centered equally in the area you've set aside for them. Sketch the words and letters out on a piece of paper, and fold the paper in half. That will give you the center point. While you can make a bunch of measurements based on the size of the letters, it is more important that the letters and names look centered. Trace the letters onto the blank, and have someone else look at it to proofread and look at the spacing. If you don't like the spacing, erase the lines and try again.

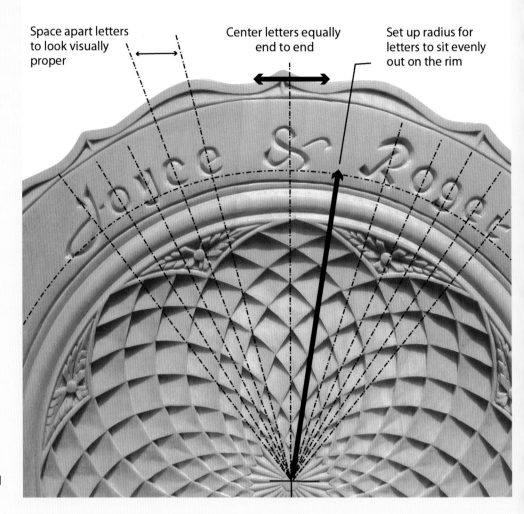

Space apart letters to look visually proper

Center letters equally end to end

Set up radius for letters to sit evenly out on the rim

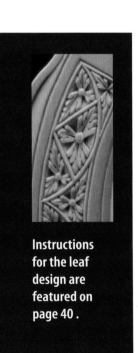

Instructions for the leaf design are featured on page 40 .

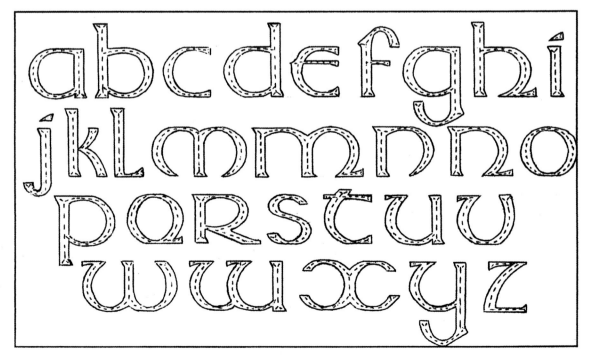

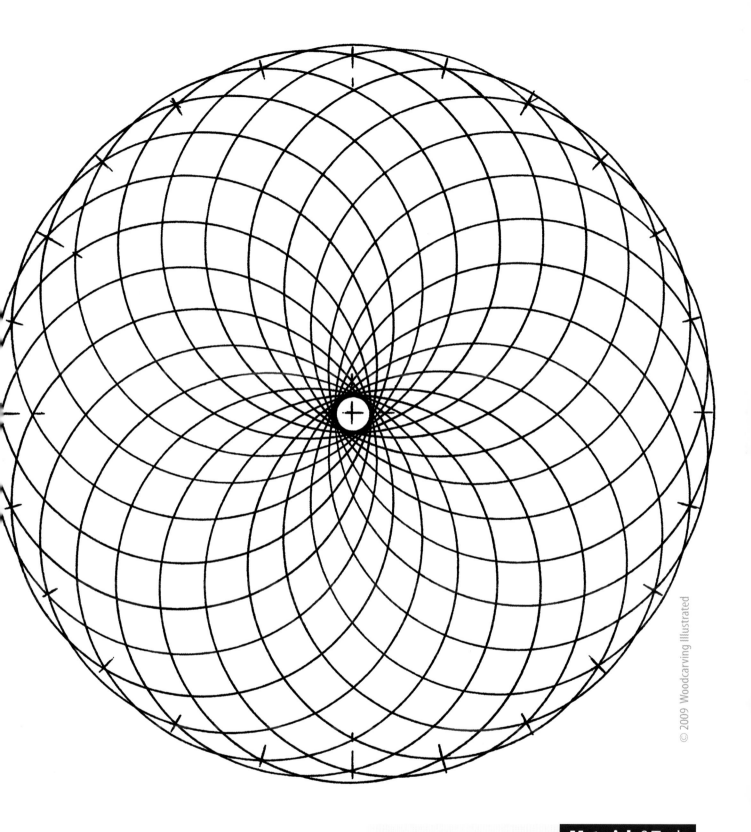

Photocopy at 130%

Materials & Tools

Materials:
- 10"-diameter basswood carving plate
- Finish of choice
- Graphite paper

Tools:
- Modified chip carving knife

Chip Carving – Wedding Plate 93

Chip Carved Letters

By Barry McKenzie

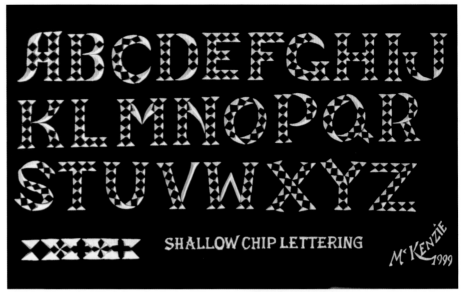

SHALLOW CHIP LETTERING

McKenzie 1999

To carve letters, you once had to choose between buying specialized tools or spending a lot of time practicing difficult cuts. These letters are simple to carve. They use standard chip-carving cuts, and they require only one tool.

These letters are pretty standard in terms of style. They are similar to either a traditional Bold Roman or Block font. My letters are filled with "blocks" that stand out, owing to the chips removed from around them.

This technique makes the areas not chip carved the most visible. Among artists, these areas are referred to as negative space.

Making a Three-Sided Chip

Most of the chips taken out in this approach require shallow-style chip carving. Three-sided in shape, they are executed with two vertical stab cuts and then a shallow slice or "ramp cut" to the front of the chip. The last cut brings together the points of all cuts. The depth of the cuts is relative to the size of the chip. The depth is about half the width of a chip; so the larger the chip, the deeper the cut.

Making Overlapping Shallow Chips

Letters and numbers consist of stems and arms. Look at the letter *T*. The vertical component is the stem and the horizontal is the arm. Since an inside right angle is created where these two parts meet, it is impossible to make a single three-sided chip to define the letter. Instead, two shallow chips are removed at right angles to each other. Think of one shallow chip blending into another shallow chip. Half of each chip takes up the same space. Letters *A, E, F, G, H, L,* and *T,* all require overlapping shallow chips.

Old-World-Style Chips

To make the spear tip-shaped parts of letters *A, B, C, D, G, J, K, M, O, P, Q, R, S, U, V,* you need to use old-world-style chips. These chips are used where you cannot place blocks surrounded by shallow chips. For an old-world-style chip, make two vertical stab cuts, just as you do with the shallow chip. Then follow up with two angular slice cuts, made to a depth and point where all cuts converge.

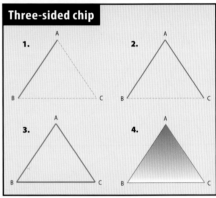

Three-sided chip

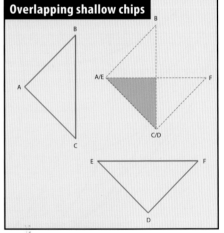

Overlapping shallow chips

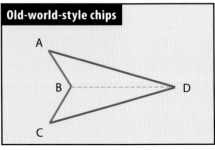

Old-world-style chips

_____ Stab cut

_____ Angled or ramp cut

Photocopy at desired size

© 2009 Woodcarving Illustrated

FINISHING NOTES

TIP

I use several coats of oil finish to finish many of my pieces. Apply the first two coats carefully, and keep the finish out of the chips. Because these coats absorb into the wood quickly, any oil inside the chips will bleed out into the surrounding areas, which makes the rims of the chips look dull. Rub the third coat over the entire piece. Since the surrounding areas have already received two coats of oil, the third coat is not as likely to bleed out into these areas from the chips.

Use caution when working with oil finishes. Rags or cloths used to apply the finish present a danger of spontaneous combustion. Dispose of wiping cloths in a sealed, water-filled container.

I paint some of my projects prior to carving. Paints work well where there is sufficient background and negative space so that the chip carved patterns stand out. Carve right through the paint for a contrast between the painted surface and natural wood.

Before painting, seal the wood with a wood sealer or pre-stain wood conditioner, available at most home centers. This prevents the paint from bleeding into the wood. Paint the blank with full-strength acrylic paint straight from the container. Never water down paint or use any that sounds sloshy when you shake the container. The goal is a thick coat on the wood. Then, simply carve through the paint.

Colorful Plaque

By John Niggemeyer

I wanted to make a special project to celebrate one of the most joyous days of my life. While many chip carvings have a natural finish, I wanted to make this plaque extra special and decided to spice it up a bit by adding some subtle colors. The process of adding acrylic paints to highlight a chip carving is actually quite simple and makes a striking difference. I also used a chip carving technique of my own design as a border for this plaque, which commemorates the birth of my only granddaughter—she really is our little angel.

This unique birth announcement was custom carved for our granddaughter, Abbey.

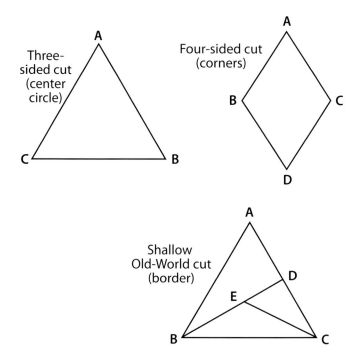

Three-sided cut (center circle)

Four-sided cut (corners)

Shallow Old-World cut (border)

Carving a modified old-world-style shallow chip

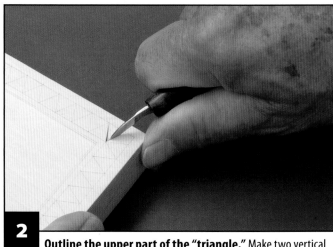

1   **Draw the border onto the piece.** Space the chips evenly around the border. My chips are 1cm wide at the base; adjust your dimensions to match your blank.

2   **Outline the upper part of the "triangle."** Make two vertical cuts into the wood. Start with the tip of your knife at point A, angling your knife down toward point B. The knife tip should cut about 1/16" into the wood, and the cut should get shallower along the length of the blade so that it doesn't cut past point B. Repeat between point A and point C.

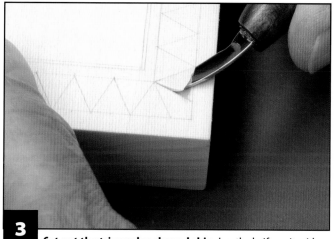

3 **Cut out the triangular-shaped chip.** Lay the knife on its side and lift the handle slightly so it lifts a shallow chip. Do not cut past the border connecting points B and D.

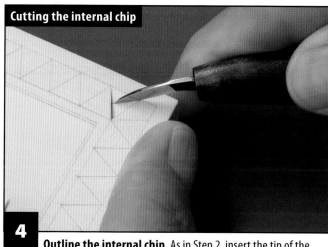

4 **Outline the internal chip.** As in Step 2, insert the tip of the knife 1/16" into the wood at point D. The knife should angle towards point B, where the depth of the cut should decrease to nothing. Recut the line between point D and point C.

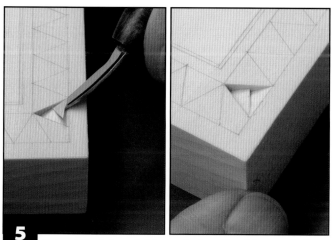

5 **Cut out the internal chip you just outlined.** Lay your knife on its side again, and press its tip into the triangle formed by the cuts made in Step 4. Be careful not to cross the border line established in Step 3.

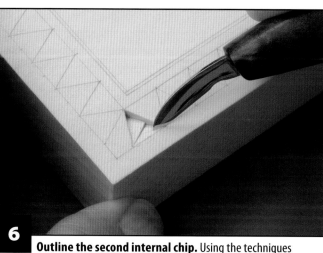

6 **Outline the second internal chip.** Using the techniques explained in the earlier steps, outline a triangle by joining point E to point C and point E to point B.

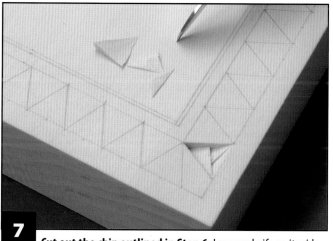

7 **Cut out the chip outlined in Step 6.** Lay your knife on its side, and press the tip into the tip of the triangle. Again, be careful not to cut past the border established in Step 3.

FINISHING THE CHIP CARVING `TIP`

After the carving is completed, it is important to remove any fingerprints and all pencil marks. I use wood cleaner that if used moderately, dries quickly and doesn't raise the grain. Take the time to clean a piece of scrap wood at the same time—that will give you a trial piece for your paint colors.

After cleaning the wood, seal it with two parts lacquer sanding sealer mixed with one part lacquer thinner. Apply it with a brush. Use the brush to push the excess out of the chips so it doesn't pool at the bottom. Allow the sealer to dry for six hours, and then apply a second coat. Treat your trial piece using the same method.

After the sealer has dried, apply three light coats of clear satin wood finish. Allow the finish to dry for 20 minutes between each coat. I apply the finish now because it makes it easier for me to clean the paint off parts I don't want painted (see Painting the Chip Carving).

Painting the Chip Carving

Start by diluting your acrylic paints according to the paint palette. This dilution will give the paints the consistency of a stain or wash and give you a muted look. You don't want much color; just enough to make the project interesting. I mix all the colors in a bubble palette.

Be sure to stir the washes right before using them, the water and acrylic pigments tend to separate quickly. After you've finished all of the painting and allowed the paint to dry, apply a few more coats of clear satin wood finish.

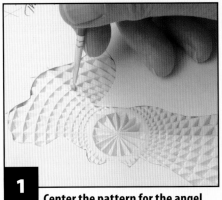

1 **Center the pattern for the angel in the circular section (which I call the swirling color wheel).** Paint the angel using the white mixture. Paint the surface of the wood as well as the inside of the carved chips. Allow the paint to dry.

2 **Using the photos as a guide,** paint one color at a time in the carved chips up to the angel. I use a #5/0 paintbrush.

3 **Use a damp cloth to wipe any paint from the surface of the carving (leaving the paint only in the carved chips).** Continue around the entire swirling color wheel using the same technique with each color. Do not paint over the white angel.

4 **Add a little color to the angel.** After you've painted the swirling color wheel, dilute the washes a little more with water. Then follow the pattern to paint only the carved chips inside the angel. If you get any paint on the top surface, wipe it away with a damp cloth.

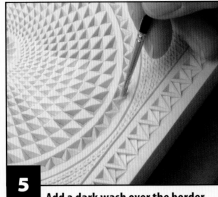

5 **Add a dark wash over the border and lettering (optional).** Dilute raw sienna with water to the consistency of skim milk, and brush this over the border and letters. This will give the illusion of deeper cuts in these sections.

Materials:

- 1" x 9" x 12" basswood plaque
- Acrylic paint: cadmium yellow, bonnie blue, white, Christmas green, tomato spice, raw sienna
- Soft rag
- Lacquer sanding sealer
- Clear satin wood finish
- Wood cleaner
- Lacquer thinner

Tools:

- Chip carving knife of choice

- Stab knife (for texture around swirling color wheel)
- Pencil
- Ruler (if drawing own pattern)
- #5/0 paintbrush
- Bubble palette

Painting Palette:

- Yellow: 3 drops cadmium yellow, 1 drop white, 1 teaspoon water
- Blue: 4 drops bonnie blue, 1 drop white, 1 teaspoon water

Materials & Tools

- Green: 3 drops Christmas green, 1 drop white, 1 teaspoon water
- Red: 2 drops tomato spice, 1 drop white, 1 teaspoon water
- White: mix the white with enough water to make the paint easy to apply (personal choice)
- Raw sienna: mix the raw sienna with water to the consistency of skim milk

Angel painting guide

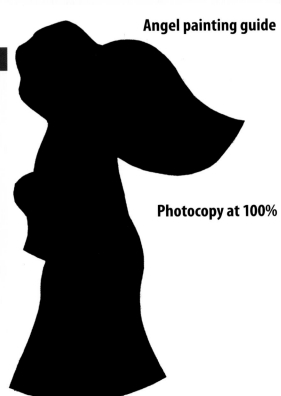

Photocopy at 100%

Photocopy at 125%

Classic Spoon Rack

By Tom Douglass

When looking at antiques, I found certain small antiques were no longer available except for very expensive originals. Since I'm a self-taught woodworker, I decided I could recreate some for a much more reasonable price.

I started out making small replicas of pipe boxes and spoon racks. My goal was to make something affordable but would also fit in with a person's existing collection. In this article, I will show you how to recreate a classic spoon rack.

I made mine using basic tools—an ordinary bench knife, a 5/16" palm chisel and a 5/16" palm skew chisel to clean out tight corners—but you can use the tools you are comfortable with. To add to the piece's authentic look, I hand planed it with a modified plane ground to produce a slightly rounded cut.

Step 1: Prepare the blank. Plane the uncut boards down with the hand plane to give it texture (if desired) and draw the pattern on.

Step 2: Cut the outlines. Outline the heart, star and swirl using the bench knife. Angling your knife inward, carve a shallow recess around the entire outline of the heart, leaving the heart protruding. Alternate between the chisel, skew chisel, and knife until you get the corners cleaned out.

Step 3: Cut similar chips out for the star and the swirl. Leave the corners of each the same level as the wood (see the pattern). This gives the two a three-dimensional feel. Also, on the star, leave the center high and just cut in triangles to give the star a 3-D feel. Alternate between the three tools until you clean out the corners.

Step 4: Carve the three-pointed star in the middle of the heart. Leave the center of the star in relief. Different sections call for the use of different tools.

Step 5: Carve the fan at the top. Start by carving a triangle deeper at the top in the center of the fan (following the pattern). Then, make a stop cut directly on the line at the next ray of the fan on both sides. Feather the cut out so it gets progressively shallower as you reach the bottom of the fan. Cut a chip out by making a cut directly at the next line angled to the stop cut. Continue until the fan is carved out in relief. The skew chisel is very important to clean out the tight, almost undercut, rays of the fan.

Step 6: Cut the dados, or grooves, for spoon racks. Use the table saw, making multiple cuts until you have a wide enough dado. If you have a router with a proper sized dado bit, you could also use that.

Step 7: Cut out the rack with the scroll saw or coping saw. I use a fine blade, but use what you are comfortable with.

Step 8: Sand all of the surfaces. Use 220-grit sandpaper until they are smooth.

Step 9: Fit the spoon holders into the dados. Secure them with wood glue. Nail them from behind to make sure they are tight.

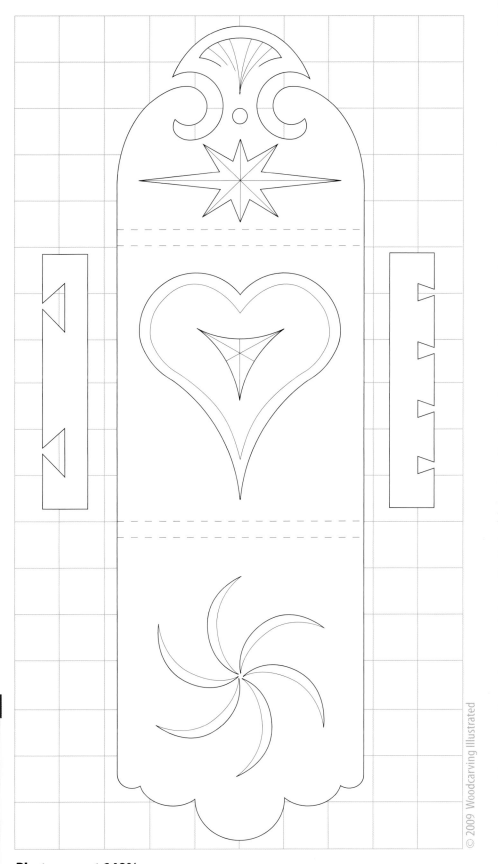

Photocopy at 140%

Materials & Tools

Materials:
- ³⁄₈" x 6" x 12" pine board
- 2 each, ³⁄₈" x 6" x 1" pine
- Small finishing nails
- Wood glue

Tools:
- Scroll saw or coping saw
- Router with dado bit or table saw
- Knife of choice
- ⁵⁄₁₆" flat palm chisel
- ⁵⁄₁₆" skew chisel
- Modified hand plane with rounded iron (optional)
- Sandpaper, 220 grit

Tom Douglass Gallery

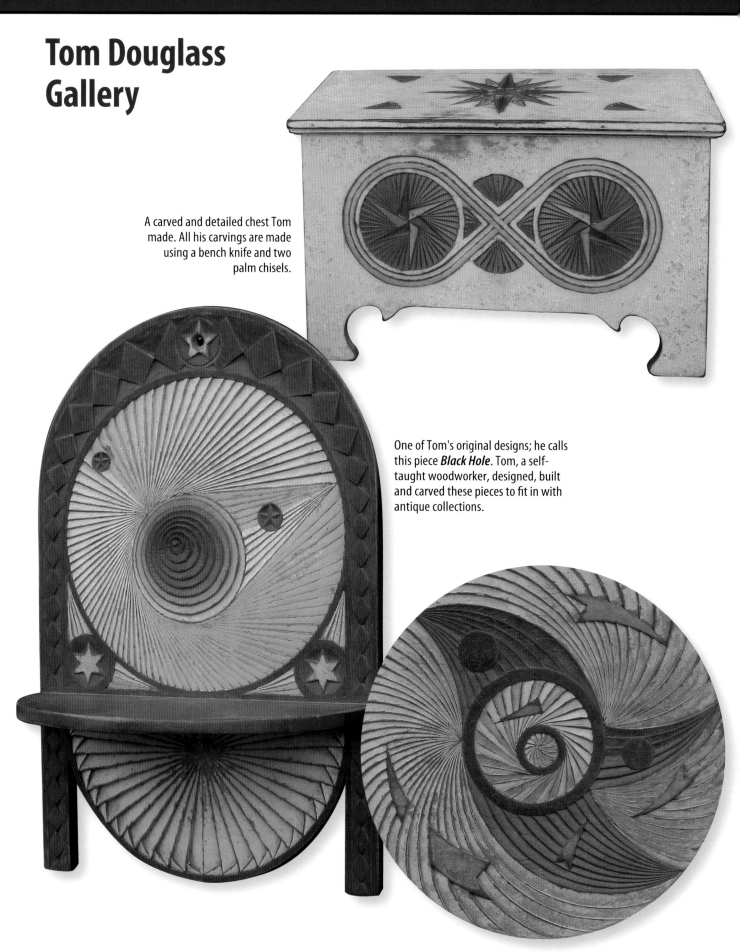

A carved and detailed chest Tom made. All his carvings are made using a bench knife and two palm chisels.

One of Tom's original designs; he calls this piece *Black Hole*. Tom, a self-taught woodworker, designed, built and carved these pieces to fit in with antique collections.

Another in Tom's series of black-hole-inspired carvings.

I developed my own way to antique my work. I painted the rack in thirds, starting with the top third.

• *Use an inexpensive latex paint. As soon as you finish each section—while the paint is still wet—run a propane torch lightly over the paint. Since the paint is still wet, the torch will make it bubble and pop. If the paint is dry, the torch will just burn the paint and you will need to paint over that spot and try again. Finish the whole rack using this technique.*

• *After painting, use 220-grit sandpaper to round over all the corners. Then, go over all of the painted surfaces to further distress the paint. The sandpaper should loosen up some of the paint bubbles, making the spoon rack look older.*

• *I also use a nut pick, used to clean the nuts out of shells, to clean out some of the paint in the chip carvings. Leave a little paint inside, but clean most of it out.*

• *Then round over all the sharp edges and clean the paint off all edges. You want the rack to look like it hung in your grandmother's kitchen for 100 years and was dusted off every day. All of the sharp corners should be sanded away.*

• *I use potassium permanganate to distress the paint and wood. Then, I use a mixture of household cleansers and flour to fill in some of the carved spaces and antique the piece further. Since the potassium permanganate is caustic, you can also just rub the whole thing with burlap to distress it further. Then, rub a little paraffin wax on the burlap and rub it again as a finish.*

A carved and detailed spoon rack. Tom uses a variety of templates to lay out his geometric designs.

A stylized shelf shaped into a female form. Tom developed a unique finishing technique to antique his pieces.

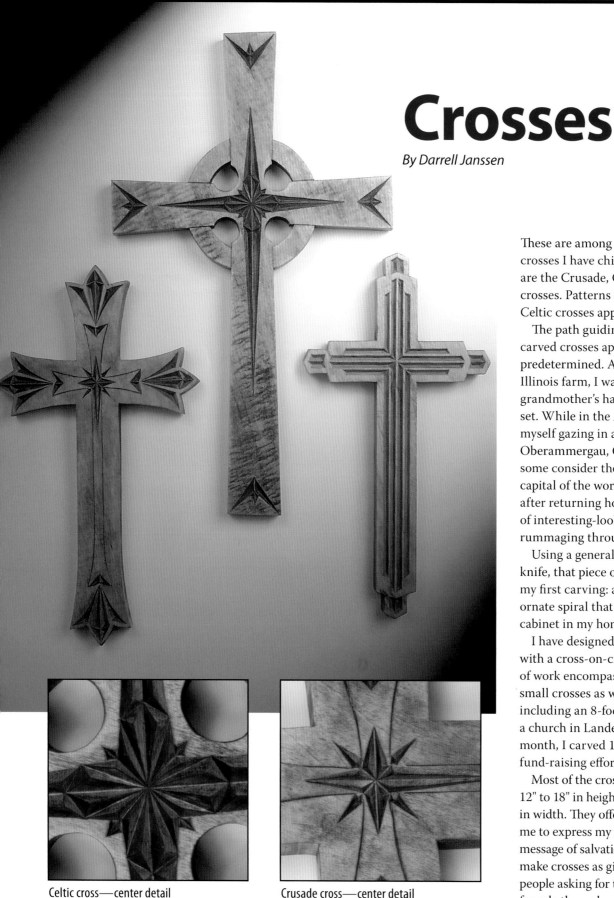

Crosses

By Darrell Janssen

These are among the hundreds of crosses I have chip carved. From left are the Crusade, Celtic, and Hope crosses. Patterns of the Crusade and Celtic crosses appear on page 106.

The path guiding me to chip carved crosses appears to have been predetermined. As a child on an Illinois farm, I was fascinated by my grandmother's hand-carved nativity set. While in the Army, I found myself gazing in awe at carvings in Oberammergau, Germany, which some consider the woodcarving capital of the world. Around 1977, after returning home, I found a piece of interesting-looking basswood while rummaging through firewood.

Using a general-purpose carving knife, that piece of basswood became my first carving: a candle stand with an ornate spiral that now sits in a display cabinet in my home.

I have designed about 35 crosses with a cross-on-cross motif. My body of work encompasses more than 250 small crosses as well as larger ones, including an 8-foot-tall altar cross for a church in Lander, Wyoming. In one month, I carved 14 crosses to support a fund-raising effort at our church.

Most of the crosses range in size from 12" to 18" in height and about half that in width. They offer a special outlet for me to express my faith and share God's message of salvation. I continue to make crosses as gifts, for benefits, or for people asking for them. They are also for sale through my part-time business (see He's Out of the Woods).

Celtic cross—center detail

Crusade cross—center detail

Darrell Janssen carved this 8' altar cross for the Bethel Lutheran Church in Lander, Wyoming.

Getting Started

I use locally cut basswood almost exclusively for the crosses. It is soft to carve, and a few small imperfections give my crosses character. I can apply any color or finish to basswood, so it is easy to match someone's home furnishings or even the décor of a church.

I begin by transferring a pattern onto ¾"-thick wood using graphite paper. Then, I cut off the portion of the board with the pattern on it, leaving margins wide enough on the outside to support my hand while carving.

Chip Carving Tips

If you are new to chip carving, I suggest that you go to shows. Looking at a variety of projects, some more complex than others, will help you decide on the type of project to undertake. I obtain suggestions from other carvers at shows and in clubs. There are classes in chip carving, usually available through carving clubs.

If it's difficult to attend a class, get a pattern, put it on the wood and practice. A book will explain how to hold your knife. You'll make mistakes, including cutting too deeply. Then, after a while, you'll do it right. It

depends on the time you put into it. Fortunately, you don't need a lot of space to chip carve; I do this in my living room on a card table.

When I carve the design in the cross, I start in the center and work my way out and around.

A magnifying light helps me see some of the longer lines on the cross, and consequently I can maintain a straighter line. I make every effort to hone my knife at least once an hour. A piece of leather mounted on a board sprinkled with sharpening compound works best.

After completing the carving, I cut away the margin with a variable-speed jigsaw. I follow that by sanding the edge using a hobby belt sander with a 1"-wide belt or a Dremel sander. My wife, Sara, usually takes over here and sands the front, back, and side surfaces with 400-grit paper to prevent the surface from absorbing too much stain. It takes me between 90 minutes and six hours to carve the smaller crosses. This does not include the time needed to transfer a pattern to the wood and to sand and stain the project.

Finishing Tips

Sara, who helps me with the finishing, seals the edges with a sanding sealer before staining. Sealing prevents the edges from becoming too dark from the stain and allows the grain to show through. For the actual carved portion, no sealer is applied because I want the stain to create a contrast. We use an oil-based stain,

His grandmother's hand-carved nativity set fascinated Darrell Janssen when he was a child growing up on an Illinois farm.

such as Minwax Golden Oak or Early American, applying it with a small artists' brush to reach the crevices and wiping it elsewhere with a discarded cotton T-shirt. The excess is wiped off to even the color on the surface. Finally, we apply a double coat of satin spray polyurethane with a light buffing between coats with 0000 steel wool. To hang the cross, I use a router to put a keyhole slot in the back. I always sign my work; you should, too.

HE'S OUT OF THE WOODS

After 15 years of carving as a hobby and focusing more on carving crosses, I established a part-time woodcarving business in 1997. My wife, Sara, aptly named the enterprise "Out of the Woods" (www.darrelljanssen.com) because that's where the material I use originates. The name also rings true to me, since each carving is hidden within the wood and has to be uncovered.

I relied on word of mouth to market my work until my daughter, Julie Ashkenazi, an art director working in catalogs, encouraged me to sell my work through exhibits. For a time, my crosses sold at a Christian bookstore near my home. Since then, I have found other locations and keep looking for new venues, such as carving shows, to display my crosses. Depending on where they are purchased, my carvings cost $40 to $100.

In 2001, I entered the Illinois Artisans Program and was selected to participate. The program allows my work to be displayed for sale at three locations in the state: the Illinois Artisans gift shop in the James R. Thompson Building in Chicago, the gift shop of the Illinois State Museum in Springfield, and the Illinois Artisans gallery and shop at Rend Lake at Whittington. Some of my crosses are also for sale at the Vesterheim Museum in Decorah, Iowa.

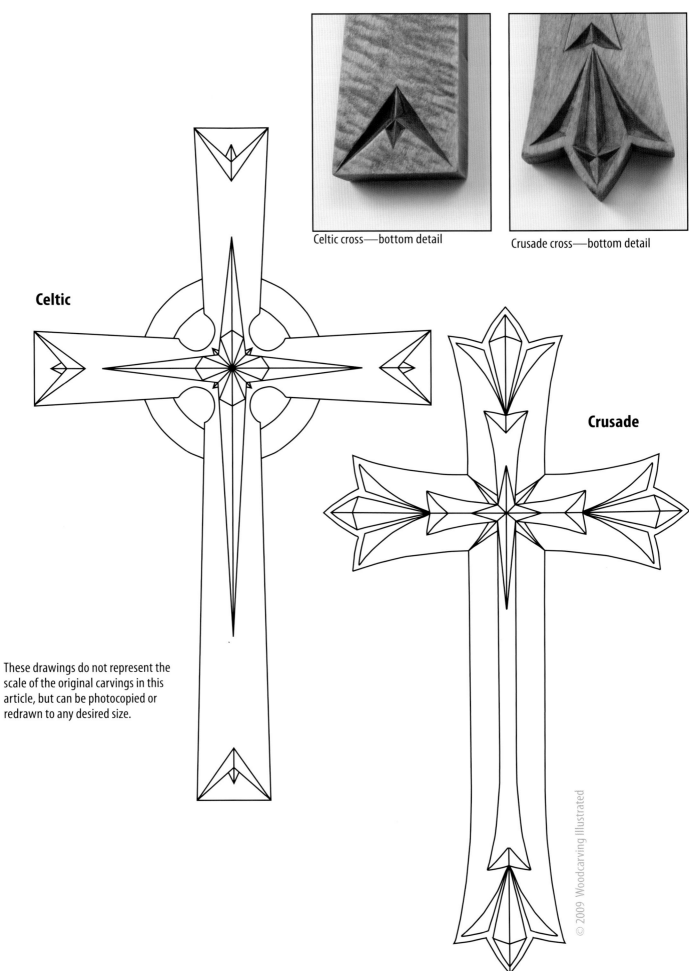

Celtic cross—bottom detail

Crusade cross—bottom detail

Celtic

Crusade

These drawings do not represent the scale of the original carvings in this article, but can be photocopied or redrawn to any desired size.

© 2009 Woodcarving Illustrated

Serving Tray

By Barry McKenzie

The chip carving on this serving tray, done through the painted surface, makes the contrast between the natural wood and the color particularly outstanding. In addition to being functional, it will enhance the décor in a room in your home, and it can even be displayed as a wall hanging. The tray also makes an outstanding gift for someone special on any occasion. With the removable bottom panel of the tray, you have an easier time of chip carving, and you may even want to put another design on the opposite side of the panel so that it can be reversed to further show off your talents. If you intend to use the tray for serving drinks, I recommend putting a piece of ¼"-thick Plexiglas over the panel to protect the paint from damage and wear.

Preparation

This basswood serving tray measures 12½" by 18½" and comes with a removable panel that measures 12½" by 15½". After lightly sanding the raw wood with 220-grit foam-core sandpaper, apply acrylic paint with a fine bristle or foam brush to one side of the panel. Do not, however, dilute the paint. It should be thick like pudding so that it sits on the top surface and does not bleed into the wood grain. Before applying a second coat of paint, lightly sand the painted surface.

I use a variety of bold colors that include a cobalt blue or a rich red. The idea is to obtain as much contrast as possible between the paint and the natural wood color that shows through the chip design. For even greater contrast, do not paint the frame of the serving tray.

If you are uncomfortable using paints, then the panel can be stained; but I don't recommend it because of wood seams. The panel consists of laminated boards glued together because wide basswood boards are not readily available. Glue lines will show through the stain, but paint hides them. Also be aware that high humidity warps a wide panel. Painting one side and sealing the wood with a varnish on the underside stabilizes the wood and reduces warping.

The finished project shows that chips were removed through the paint for a stunning contrast of natural wood and bold color. For even greater contrast, the frame of the tray was left its natural color.

Transferring the Pattern

White transfer paper, available at art and craft stores, works best for putting the pattern on the painted wood. The white lines created by the paper are easy to erase from the painted surface or they can be removed with a damp rag. Once you have the transfer side facing the wood and centered, securely tape it in place. Center the pattern over the transfer paper and tape that to the wood.

The final step has you laying down a sheet of ordinary household wax paper over the pattern. Tracing lines are clearly visible on the surface of the wax paper, and you will not have to lift up the pattern and transfer paper to see what lines are missing. Tape down the wax paper so that it does not move.

Before chip carving, remove the wax paper, pattern, and transfer paper. Be aware that the white lines created by the transfer paper will smudge. You may want to lay some wax paper over areas where the knife hand will come in contact with the wood.

A basswood tray with a removable bottom panel is an excellent choice for a chip carved project.

Use a tracing stylus or an inkless fine or medium ballpoint pen for tracing. Drafting devices such as a straightedge ruler, circle template, or French curve make tracing neater and straighter than tracing freehand.

Chip Carving

The pattern consists of different styles of chip carving including geometric, free form, Swedish shallow cuts, and Old-World-Style. Take note that a space or ribbon of paint exists between each chip, unlike traditional chip carving that has chips adjacent to each other. In most cases, the space helps to eliminate breakouts between chips. It also isolates the chip in the design for more visible recognition within the pattern.

Keeping the Cutting Edge Sharp

Even though the layer of paint is nearly microscopic in thickness, it will still dull the cutting edge of your knife. The trade-off is that while the finished product is a beautiful contrast between the natural color of the wood and the paint, you will have to touch up the edge of the blade frequently. Even more problematic to a cutting edge is metallic paint. The particles of metal can damage the knife blade, requiring major re-sharpening.

Finish Coat

It is advisable to apply a finish coat to the tray frame and panel to protect both the paint and the natural wood. A water-based finish is the best choice on painted surfaces. Non-water-based products will turn the natural wood to a honey yellow color, reducing or diminishing the contrast between the lightly colored basswood and the paint.

Photocopy at 165%

Mangle Board

By Barry McKenzie

The horse I carved as a handle for this mangle board was stylized; a wood carver may want to detail it more than I did. Trace the pattern onto the wood using graphite transfer paper. Put a layer of wax paper over the pattern—that way you can see where you have already traced. Trace lightly so you don't dent the wood, and touch up any missing lines with a pencil later. By the way, my wife, with a smile, would not accept the mangle board I carved for her until I permanently carved her name and date onto it (see The Story of the Mangle Board, at right).

Materials & Tools

Materials:
- Wood of choice, size of choice
- Graphite transfer paper
- Wax paper (optional)
- Red pen (optional)
- Tape
- Finish of choice
- Stain of choice

Tools:
- Chip carving knife of choice
- Brush or rag (for applying finish

THE STORY OF THE MANGLE BOARD

Scandinavian "mangletre" (mangle boards) are traditionally embellished with what I call old-world-style chip carving. A wooden dowel was rolled under the board to press water out of linen before hanging it to dry.

According to my sources, mangle boards were carved by young suitors and presented to a potential betrothed, somewhat like an engagement ring is presented today. If the young lady accepted the carving that already had her name and date carved on it, the suitor was accepted as a suitable husband (assuming he was already approved by the lady's father). The abstract Norwegian Fjord horse/pony acts as a handle for the mangle board.

Today, mangle boards are used mostly as a wall decoration. These chip carving patterns were designed by Jan Hulsebos of Wilhelminaoord, Netherlands, who taught at the Barry McKenzie School for Chip Carving in 2004.

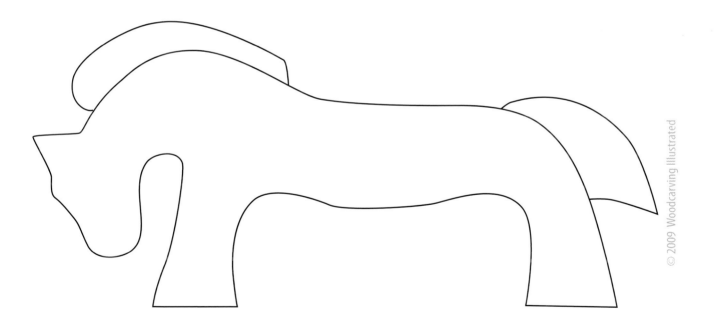

Size to fit blank of choice

© 2009 Woodcarving Illustrated

Layout
guide

Size to fit blank of choice

Rosette

By Dennis Moor

This rosette-inspired design can be traced onto a blank using graphite transfer paper, but with a few basic tools, it's easy to draw it—or customize it—yourself. Use a mechanical pencil with .5mm lead and a compass to get yourself started. Once you have your basic techniques down, experiment a little with the pencil and compass to develop your own designs.

Size to fit blank of choice

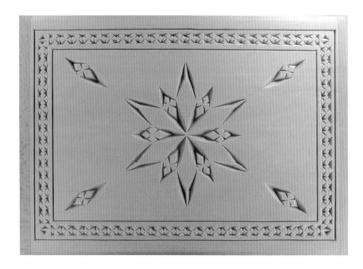

This jewelry box lid is decorated with the rosette and a simple border.

Materials & Tools

Materials:

- Wood of choice at size of choice
- Graphite transfer paper
- Mechanical pencil with .5mm lead
- Compass
- Red pen (optional)
- Tape
- Finish of choice
- Stain of choice

Tools:

- Chip carving knife of choice
- Brush or rag (for applying finish)

Dove Peace Cross

By Dennis Moor

This beginner pattern was carved in basswood. You could also choose to carve it in butternut. The pattern is simple enough that you can draw it directly onto the blank. If you don't feel comfortable drawing it, trace the design onto tracing paper, place graphite transfer paper under the tracing paper, and trace it onto the blank. *Do not* use carbon paper; carbon paper leaves waxy lines that are impossible to erase.

Size to fit blank of choice

Materials & Tools

Materials:
- Basswood or wood of choice at size of choice
- Graphite transfer paper
- Mechanical pencil with .5mm lead
- Red pen (optional)
- Tape
- Finish of choice
- Stain of choice

Tools:
- Chip carving knife of choice
- Brush or rag (for applying finish)

The hinged front panel opens for easy cleaning and secures with a simple gate hook.

Stylish Birdhouse

By Barry McKenzie

With the classically shingled roof and brilliant, stylized chip carving, you might be hesitant to hang this birdhouse outdoors. But returning songbirds will reward your generosity with their cheerful presence, and the project is actually weather resistant.

The birdhouse is fairly simple to construct. In fact, more than 50 of them were completed by students in my classes last year. Most of the students chose this bird by a fence post design. The bottom of the house has a gate hook to keep the hinged front from being opened by a predator or pushed out by too much nesting material inside.

The roof is at a 12° slope for water run-off, and the shingles, while easy to carve, make an impressive display. This form of chip carving is called stylized free-form, which is not as precise as geometric chip carving. Chip carving through paint does have a tendency to dull the knife's cutting edge a little faster, so I strop more often. The design could easily be carved in shallow relief if you prefer. I assemble my birdhouses using only exterior weatherproof glue on the joints because brads always seem to fall exactly where a chip is going. The interior cavity of the birdhouse is left natural wood.

The chart below lists the entrance hole sizes for various species of songbirds. The chart also includes notes for how far above the ground the birdhouse should be mounted.

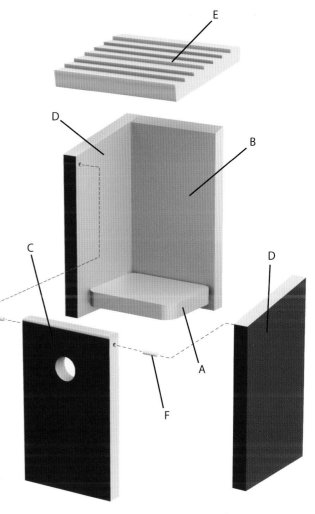

Birdhouse specifications for different species

Bird Species	Entrance Hole	Mounting Height
Chickadee	1⅛"-diameter	6'
Tufted Titmouse, Nuthatch	1¼"-diameter	6'
Blue Bird, House Wren	1½"-diameter	6'
Swallow	1½"-diameter	10'
House Finch	2"-diameter	8'
Purple Martin	2½"-diameter	15'

BIRDHOUSE BASICS

• *I didn't add a perch because I've read that predators use the perch more often than songbirds. I have seen nesting birds fly straight into the hole and exit the same way.*

• *Clean out the birdhouse in early spring before the migrating birds return. Before opening the birdhouse, make sure nobody has taken up residence. I have seen several bluebirds share a birdhouse over a mild winter. I also have one flying squirrel that has made a permanent home in one of my birdhouses. It was a big surprise to both of us when I tried to clean out the bedding material and found a wide-eyed flying squirrel looking back at me!*

Carving shingles

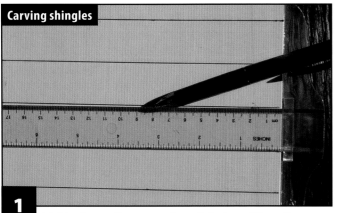

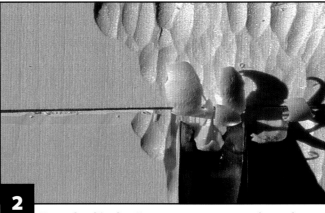

1 **Divide the roof into rows.** Draw six horizontal lines, 1" apart, across the width of the roof to make seven rows of shingles. Make a deep cut along these lines with a chip carving knife to outline the front edge of each shingle. It may take a few passes to reach a depth of at least ³⁄₃₂". It is impossible to go too deep.

2 **Taper the shingles.** Use a gouge to remove wood up to the vertical cuts made in step 1. Taper the shingles so it looks like the lower shingle disappears beneath the edge of the one above it. Feel free to deepen the stop cut as you go. Work across each row before moving on to the next. The depth is up to you.

3 **Divide the rows into individual shingles.** Each row of shingles is staggered in relation to the row above it. Start with a shingle width of about ¾", and vary the width from there. Do not make every shingle the same width. Cut along these lines with a chip carving knife to divide the rows into individual shingles.

4 **Outline the thickness of the shingles.** Carve a line along the bottom and sides of the shingles to represent the thickness. This gives the illusion that each shingle is individually carved. Since each row is tapered, it will look like the individual shingles are tapered. Do not sand the shingles smooth.

BIRDHOUSE CONSTRUCTION NOTES

- *The dimensions will change if you use wood thinner than ¾".*
- *Use basswood, butternut, or white cedar; more dense wood is difficult to chip carve.*
- *Paint the exterior surfaces of the birdhouse with a dark acrylic paint (I use hunter green).*
- *Use an exterior protective spray spar urethane on the exterior surfaces.*
- *Drill holes for dowels at least ½" deep.*
- *Place the two hinge dowels in the front piece before assembling.*
- *The dowels can be up to ⁵⁄₁₆" in diameter.*

- *See the chart (page 117) for entrance hole sizes for different bird species.*
- *A safety gate hook and eye latch can be found in most hardware stores.*
- *If using thin nails, note where the chip carved pattern is located.*
- *Use exterior weather-resistant glue instead of nails, and clamp the pieces together until the glue dries.*
- *To accommodate the latch, the sides are not flush with the bottom part (A).*
- *The top of the front piece (C) has rounded edges to clear the underside of the roof when you swing it open.*

Measured drawings—use as reference, not as patterns

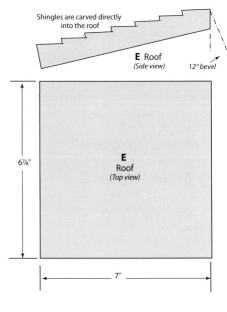

Shingles are carved directly into the roof

E Roof
(Side view)

12° bevel

6⁷⁄₈"

E Roof
(Top view)

7"

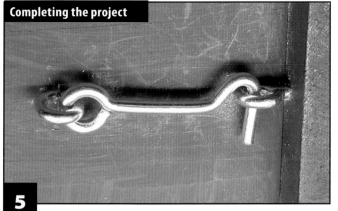

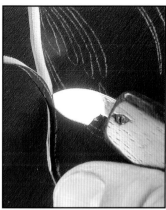

5 **Mount the gate hook.** Screw the eyelet into the front (C), just below the bottom (A). Do not screw the eyelet in the whole way; that way you can adjust the fit of the hook after you attach it to the bottom (A). Screw the hook in place, and test the fit. If the hook fits loosely, tighten up the eyelet screwed into the front (C) until the hook holds tightly.

6 **Chip carve the design.** Transfer the design to the painted birdhouse using light-colored graphite paper. Cut along one side of the pattern line, angling the knife in so the cut ends at the center of the chip to be removed. Flip the birdhouse around and cut in toward the center from the other side to free the chip. Make sure the lines are smooth and even.

Materials:

- ¾" x 4" x 5" basswood Part A (bottom)
- ¾" x 5" x 8¹⁵⁄₁₆" basswood Part B (rear)
- ¾" x 5" x 7⅞" basswood Part C (front)
- 2 each ¾" x 5½" x 8¹⁵⁄₁₆" basswood Part D (sides, top angles from 7⅞" up to 8¹⁵⁄₁₆")
- ¾" x 7" x 6⅞" basswood Part E (roof)
- 2 each ¼"–⁵⁄₁₆"-diameter x 1" dowels Part F (dowel hinges, do not glue in place)
- 2"-long gate hook set Part G (secures the front)

Materials & Tools

- Exterior weather-resistant glue
- Dark acrylic paint of choice
- Spray exterior spar urethane

Tools:

- Chip carving knife of choice
- Gouge of choice
- Ruler
- Mechanical pencil
- Paintbrushes of choice

B
Rear
(Rear view)

Beveled 12°

Rear
(Side view)

8¹⁵⁄₁₆"

5"

C
Front
(Side view)
Round off
top edges

Measured drawings—use as reference, not as patterns

F Dowels

7⁄16"

3⁄8"

Top edge 12° slope

¼" diameter blind hole, ½" min. deep (typical in Front **C**)

¼"
blind
hole

½" min.

7⅞"

C
Front
(Front view)

Hole centered on width.
See chart for entrance diameter hole size.

6"

7⅞"

D
Side - Left shown
(Cut 2)
Right and left sides are mirror images of each other.

8¹⁵⁄₁₆"

⅝" max.

Location of Bottom **A**

G Hidden latch area

5½"

5"

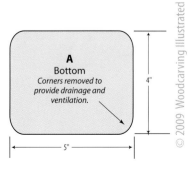

A
Bottom
Corners removed to provide drainage and ventilation.

4"

5"

© 2009 Woodcarving Illustrated

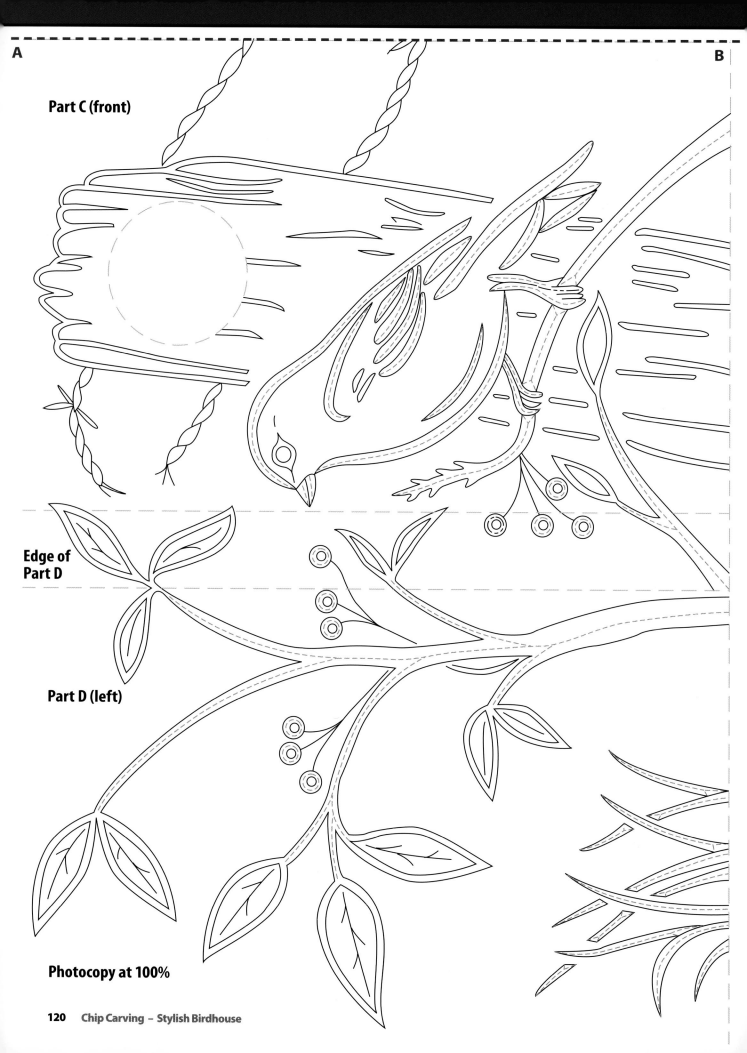

A

B

Part C (front)

**Edge of
Part D**

Part D (left)

Photocopy at 100%

Edge of Part D

A

B

Teapot Clock

Charming clock with chip carved details is perfect for the kitchen

By Barry McKenzie

This clock combines woodworking, woodcarving, and chip carving—for me it is the best of all three worlds!

The shape comes from one of the teapots in my wife's collection. The traditional carving on this piece is mainly rounding the edges of the teapot to resemble a real teapot. There is also chip carving on the teapot and the clock face. The spoon pendulum is also carved and shaped, but the spoon is embellished with more chip carving. The general woodworking comes into play when you are fitting the pendulum clockworks into the back of the clock.

Carving the Spoon

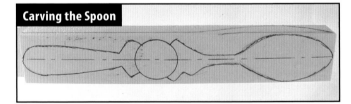

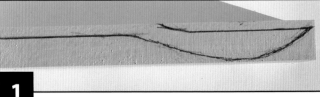

1 **Transfer the pattern to the blank.** Mark the centerline of the spoon blank and use that line to position the top view pattern. Trace the top and side profile of the spoon pattern onto the blank. When positioning the side view pattern, align the spoon handle with the top surface of the blank.

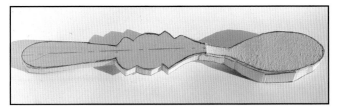

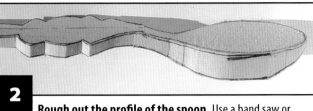

2 **Rough out the profile of the spoon.** Use a band saw or coping saw. It is also possible to carve the spoon to shape, but it will take longer. Transfer the centerline onto the top and back of the spoon blank.

Carving the bowl

3 **Carve the bottom of the spoon bowl first.** Incorporate a ridge of wood into the bowl to strengthen the part where the bowl connects to the stem. I learned this technique from love spoon carver Kenneth Bengtsson of Varberg, Sweden.

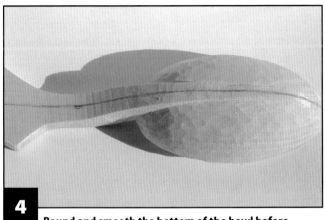

4 **Round and smooth the bottom of the bowl before hollowing the front.** Keep both sides of the centerline symmetrical. Sand away the knife marks for a finished look.

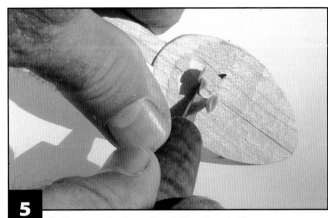

5 **Hollow out the front bowl.** Use a bent knife or a rotary power carver. Leave the walls of the bowl about 1⁄16"-thick. Smooth away the tool marks with sandpaper.

Carving the handle

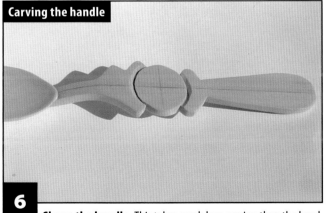

6 **Shape the handle.** This takes much less carving than the bowl. Shape it to fit your hand comfortably; this may or may not be symmetrical, but what feels good will look good. Do not remove the centerline.

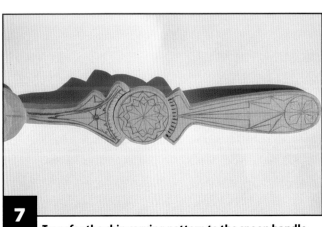

7 **Transfer the chip carving pattern to the spoon handle.** You can trace the pattern onto the wood, but I get better results by using a ruler to mark and draw the lines directly onto the spoon blank.

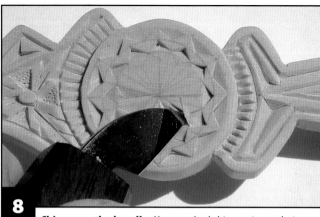

8 **Chip carve the handle.** Use standard chip carving techniques. For the leaf designs, see step 14 or page 40. The spoon is actually an attractive project all by itself, and is a great way to practice your chip carving techniques. You can follow my design or create one of your own.

For the leaf designs, see step 14 or page 40.

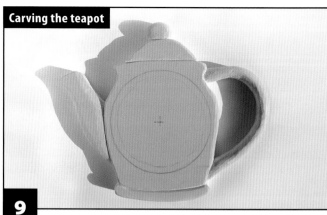

Carving the teapot

9 **Shape the teapot.** Transfer the pattern to the blank, and cut it out using your saw of choice. Shape the base, spout, lid, and handle using a carving knife. Mark the center of the teapot body and drill the appropriate-sized hole for your clock movement. Follow the instructions that come with the clock mechanism.

10 **Prepare the blank for the clock movement.** Recess an area in the back for your clock mechanism. You can use a router or hand tools. I drilled an additional recess with a Forstner bit to accommodate a rubber washer to dampen the ticking of the clock.

11 **Detail the front of the teapot.** Finish up any shaping needed, then transfer and carve the chip carving designs to the teapot body. For better adhesion, use an awl to add texture to the area where the clock face will be attached with glue.

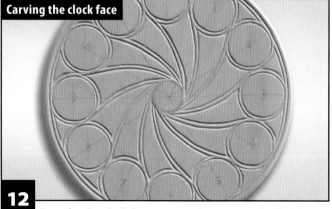

Carving the clock face

12 **Transfer the clock face pattern.** Draw or trace the clock face pattern onto the round blank. Use a chip carving knife to make the outline cuts around the different design elements.

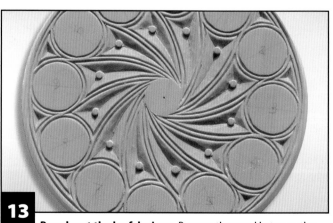

13 **Rough out the leaf designs.** Remove the wood between the line cuts in the leaf design areas. Stop cut around the buttons in the leaf designs or use an appropriate-size eye punch. If you break one off, glue it back in place.

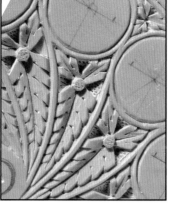

14 **Carve the leaf designs.** Cut notches to divide the section into one long leaf and two short leaves. Notch the edges of the leaves for a realistic look. Use a stab knife to add a hint of a vein to each leaf. Texture the negative spaces and buttons in the leaves.

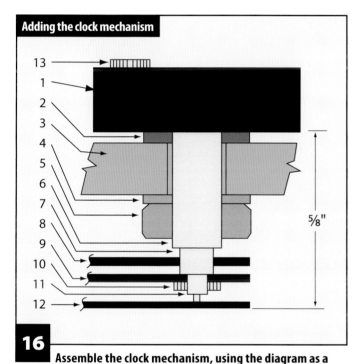

16 **Assemble the clock mechanism, using the diagram as a guide.** Mount the minute hand (9) temporarily on the shaft first. Lightly tighten the nut (10), and rotate the minute hand, using the knob (13), until it is exactly over the 12. Remove the nut and minute hand, and then mount the hour hand (8) over a full hour. Remount the minute hand and nut. Tighten the nut by holding down the time set knob on the back of the mechanism and turning the nut. Set the proper time, using the time set knob on the back. DO NOT rotate the hands to set the time. Finally, mount the second hand.

Key to Diagram

1. Clock Movement
2. Rubber Washer
3. Wood Thickness
4. Flat Washer
5. Hex Nut
6. Clock Movement Hand Shaft
7. Teflon Shaft
8. Hour Hand
9. Minute Hand
10. Minute Hand Threaded Nut
11. Thread Shaft End
12. Second Hand
13. Time Set Knob

15 **Add the numerals and attach the clock face.** Add the numbers using standard letter-carving techniques. Glue the clock face in place, and re-drill the hole for the clock mechanism. Then, apply your finish of choice. I suggest a spray lacquer.

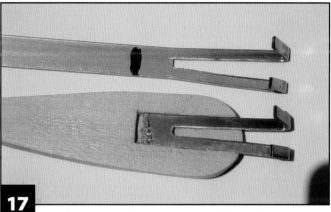

17 **Test fit the pendulum.** Hang the pendulum mechanism to determine where the spoon should hang. Mark the location. Cut the pendulum rod so that about 1⅜" of it will overlap the spoon. Carve a groove on the back of the spoon tight enough to hold the pendulum rod in place. Squeeze the tangs of the pendulum rod hanger together to fit it into the spoon groove. Make the groove slightly longer than the pendulum rod to allow for adjustment.

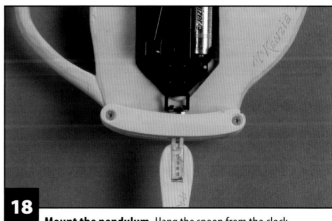

18 **Mount the pendulum.** Hang the spoon from the clock mechanism. I add a spacer flush with the clock mechanism hanger, to keep the clock hanging vertical on the wall.

Materials:

- ¾" x 1⅜" x 8⅜" basswood (spoon)
- ¾" x 8" x 10" basswood (teapot body)
- ¼" x 4½"-diameter basswood circle (clock face)
- Clock mechanism with pendulum
- Sandpaper, 220 grit
- Finish of choice
- Wood glue of choice

Tools:

- Carving knife

Materials&Tools

- Chip carving knife
- Stab knife
- Bent knife or rotary power carver of choice
- Band saw or coping saw
- Drill with assorted size drill bits
- Ruler, compass, and mechanical pencil (to draw chip carving pattern)
- Eye punch (optional)

EXTRA SPOONS

TIP

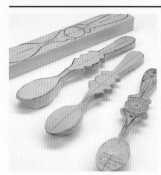

Work on several spoons at the same time. Then, if one isn't turning out the way you'd like, you have a backup.

Photocopy at 120%

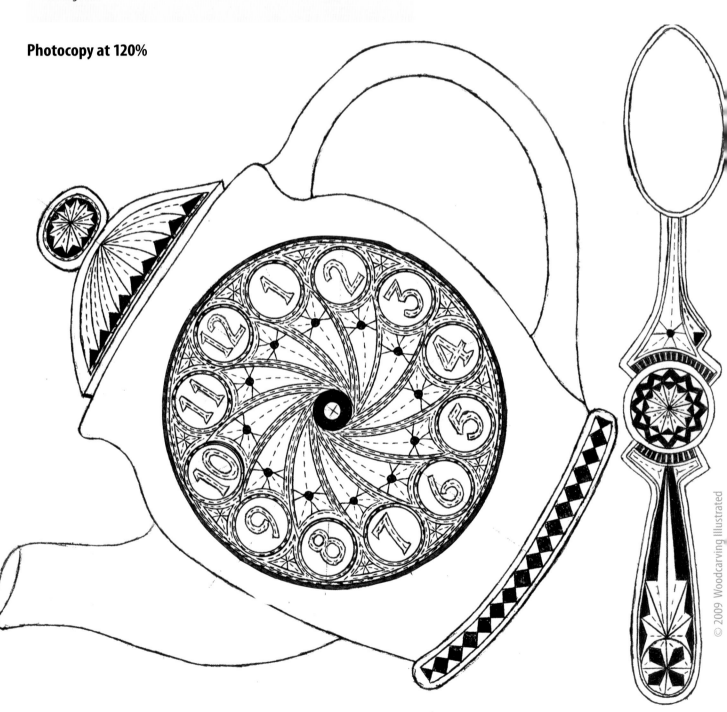

Contributors

Sharon Braunberger
Sharon has been carving and teaching carving for more than 10 years.

Tom Douglass
Tom lives in Hopwood, Pa., and has designed and built more than 900 original re-creations in his style. *www.traditionalfolkart.com/artist/decorative%3Cbr%3E%20accesories/tom_douglass/89.html*

Elaine Dugan
Elaine, of West Des Moines, Iowa, is called the golf ball lady and has appeared in Barry McKenzie's newsletter.

Diane Harto
Diane lives in Beachwood, N.J., and is a carving instructor.

Darrell Janssen
Darrell has been carving for more than 25 years and is a member of the Illinois Artisans Program.

Barry McKenzie
Barry publishes a quarterly newsletter, "Chip Carver's Newsletter." *www.chipcarvingschool.com*

Dennis Moor
Dennis owns Chipping Away and teaches chip carving classes at his store. *www.chippingaway.com*

Roger Nancoz
Roger, who lives in North Babylon, N.Y., has been carving for nearly a decade and is a full-time chip carver and instructor.

John Niggemeyer
John, of Heath, Ohio, carves a variety of subjects and has designed his own three-part chip carving.

Roger Strautman
Roger, of Woodburn, Ind., has been chip carving for nearly a decade and is an award-winning chip carver. *www.carvingsbyroger.com*

Linda Tudor
Linda has carvings in Illinois State Museum shops and works part-time in the medical field. *home.earthlink.net/~tudorart*

Index

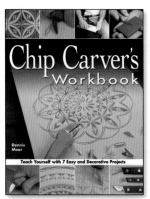
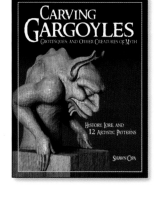
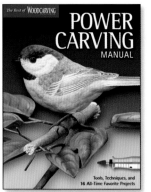
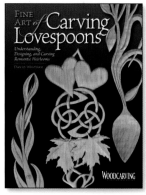
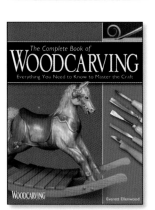